T0121767

Once There Were Dreams

Art Dickerson

Order this book online at www.trafford.com
or email orders@trafford.com

Most Trafford titles are also available at major online book retailers.

Printed in the United States of America.

ISBN: 978-1-4669-9471-3 (sc)
ISBN: 978-1-4669-9470-6 (hc)
ISBN: 978-1-4669-9472-0 (e)

Library of Congress Control Number: 2013908819

Trafford rev. 05/13/2013

www.trafford.com

North America & international
toll-free: 1 888 232 4444 (USA & Canada)
phone: 250 383 6864 • fax: 812 355 4082

INTRODUCTION

This is a historical narrative that grew out of the author's genealogical research on his great-grandfather and great-grandmother. The people who appear in the narrative were real persons, with the exception of John Bletchley, who represents the views and actions of several Confederate officers of English extraction.

The narrative calls heavily on the operations record of Confederate and Union correspondence, an extensive file of over a million pages, which Cornell University has made available on the Internet. Also used are the service records of Capt. Otto Schnaubert from the National Archives. Where prices of food or goods are mentioned, the source is either newspapers of the times or government requisitions. The citations of business in Indianola, Texas, are from the port records of that city.

The persons in the narrative eat a diet based on the availability of foodstuff during the civil war. This availability varied greatly from one location to another because transportation in the Confederate states was distinctly limited as the war progressed. The recipes are based on the author's hunting and fishing experience in Matagorda Bay and on preparation methods passed down by family members born in the nineteenth century.

It is hoped the reader will enjoy exploring the dreams and indomitable spirit of ordinary people who lived in extraordinary times in a place that no longer exists.

PART I

CHAPTER ONE

A constant breeze blows unseasonably warm and loaded with humidity. It ruffles the tufts of saw grass that line the edges of the gun port in the tiny Fort Washington. The movement of the grass dislodges a steady stream of sand, which falls at the feet of a man whose eyes sight down the barrel of a twenty-four-pounder cannon pointing seaward. In the glare of the sun, sweat runs from his gray cap to his nose, where a drop forms and falls to the breech of the cannon. To seaward, broadside on, sails a Union sloop blockading the entrance to Matagorda Bay and the port of Indianola, Texas. When the ship is two lengths short of his sight line, the man palms the cord and handle of the firing lock. When the ship's bow touches the sight line, the man steps back to the right and turns his body, pulling the cord.

The huge explosion of the firing sends shorebirds screaming down the beach. A flight of ducks rises from a cove on the shoreward side of the island, wheels overhead, and flies noisily to shore. Momentarily, the man sees the shot as a small black dot rising over the smoke, then falling toward the ship in its brief flight. Through field glasses, he sees a white spout of water on the near side of the ship. Without thought, he taps the handle of the elevating screw to raise the muzzle a fraction.

The gun crew performs a well-rehearsed ballet, swabs the barrel, clears the breech, and scours the touchhole. The man directs the movement of the gun carriage, correcting the aim for the next shot. Down the line, a second and then a third gunfire. The shorebirds, which returned after the first shot, give up and fly far down the beach. A fourth gun fires, and his crew reloads the muzzle and prepares the firing lock.

After the first shot, the Union ship turns seaward, a reasonable attempt to escape, but a move that simplifies the gunners' task. Now the entire ship is in line with the trajectory of the shells, and range matters less. Any shot lined up will hit something on board. The cord is pulled again. The black dot descends on the ship and tears the aft rigging before smashing on the deck amidships. Cheers rise from the narrow embrasure and are taken up by the other gun crews.

In quick succession, two other guns put shot aboard the ship, which completes its turn and sails at an angle to the shore, quickly adding range from the fort's guns. After a total of twelve shots, a shout of "cease firing" announces that the sloop is out of range. It is shortly after noon, December 7, 1861, and the tiny fort has won its first engagement.

Lt. Otto Schnaubert, who fired the first gun, calls out, "Secure the powder and close up the caisson." Otto is of average size, but erect carriage and broad shoulders make him appear larger. He removes his cap and wipes sweat from his brow. The wind ruffles his straw-colored hair. During the shooting, he is intently focused on the firing problem. Now, with the gun secure and adrenaline running, his stomach muscles clench. Anger floods within him. *Damn them*, he thinks. *Where do they get the right to interrupt our lives and ruin our livelihood with their blockade? We did nothing to them, and here they are threatening us, controlling our lives, and pressing hunger on our families.*

Captain Reuss, the artillery company commander, smiles broadly at Otto and taps him on the shoulder, saying, "That was damn fine shooting. You haven't forgotten what you learned in four years with the U.S. Artillery, but now you look like you're ready to eat them alive."

The voice makes Otto realize he is squeezing the iron rim on the wheel of the gun carriage until his hand turns white. He puts the hand in a pocket, saying, "Thank you, sir. It's too bad we had to stop shooting, but they were at extreme range, and we really don't have ammunition to waste."

Reuss considers that and appreciates that his decision to stop firing is endorsed by the more experienced Schnaubert. "Think about it, Otto, we fired more shells in those six minutes than our total supply when we formed this company seven months ago." Curbing his inclination to curse politicians who started wars before considering the stock of ammunition and supplies, Reuss resumes, "I want you to take this telescope and go down to the lighthouse. See what you can learn about that ship and any damage we've done."

Otto answers with a simple "Yes, sir" and turns to Sgt. John Noll, saying, "Get Will Moore and meet me at the lighthouse."

* * *

The lighthouse is only two hundred yards from the fort. The soft sands of the dunes make it seem much farther. The soil on the beach is broken shell and sand firmly packed, but the dunes are loose sand held together by saw grass. The long grass strands rip at his pant legs and score his boots. That is an aggravation; the boots are an item of pride, dating from his days as a surveyor for the future railroad spur to Indianola. The blockade caused cancellation of even that project. He keeps the boots well oiled against the day he might again work as a surveyor. Today, that seems an impossible point in a distant future.

At the lighthouse, joined by Noll and Moore, he says, "Will, you're a sailor, and you understand better than I what can be seen through this glass. I want you to relieve the lookout and tell me what you can of the Union sloop." The man on lookout comes down, and Moore takes over. Otto lifts a message pad from his pocket, and as Moore calls out, he writes:

December 7, 1861

Sloop is anchored 3 miles off. Mainsail is down. Do not see pump water on this side, so we have not likely holed the hull. Masts and spars appear unharmed.

Lt. O. L. Schnaubert

John Noll takes the message back to Captain Reuss. Otto climbs the lighthouse ladder. The cast-iron rungs feel cold and rough against his hands as he hurries sixty feet to the top. He climbs, thinking of their position. New Orleans and Galveston are blockaded by Union ships. Indianola now assumes importance as a route to get cotton to Mexico and return with arms and ammunition. That attracts more Union blockade ships to Pass Cavallo, the entry point to Indianola. The tiny Fort Washington, with its twenty-four-pounders, covers the entire width of the pass, protecting this route, but makes a prime target of itself.

He squeezes onto the narrow catwalk atop the structure. "That was a good report, Will, brief, factual, and to the point. Now tell me what you noticed about the ship before and during the shooting. Was it well handled?"

Moore, who is tall, lean, and black haired, served as a crewman on the ship of Dan Shea, who now commands the fort. He is a seaman and the son of a ship captain. "It was very well handled, Mr. Schnaubert. When it tacked, it was quick and smooth with no lost motion. That's a well-trained crew and a knowledgeable captain. He sailed up and down in front of us all morning about three miles off shore. Then on that last tack, he changed and moved inshore to about one and a half miles."

"Was that a good maneuver?"

"He did that going downwind, so he could come around on a broad reach and sail seaward when the firing started. That change, of course, was quick—it was no accident. He must have had his crew standing by on the mainsail sheets all the way in. Of course that turn made our shooting easier, but it was his best move, and in five minutes, he was out of range."

Otto considers that. "You're telling me that approach was all carefully planned in advance?"

"Yes sir, of that, I'm sure. What I can't say is why he did it. Maybe he was just trying to see what range we would start firing and how well we could shoot. If that was the case, I think he found out. We did not hurt him badly, but he has some repair work to do and likely some casualties. I have to admit, that was a brave thing."

Otto takes the glass and scans the ship, chiefly so he could later say he had personally examined it. His initial judgment proved right. Moore clearly saw what he would have missed. Well, that's the difference between a sailor and a landlubber. He thinks with a smile, *Thank God we have both.*

* * *

Arriving back at the fort, Otto finds that Daniel Shea has called a conference of senior officers for 5:00 p.m. Shea's command includes the two Indianola artillery companies and an infantry company from the nearby town of Lavaca. The conference will take place in a small dugout enclosure under a ceiling of timber with three feet of sand on top. An open side faces away from the sea. Its primary purpose is to provide cover for the command post during any shelling of the fort from ships of the Union blockade. It also serves as headquarters and hospital.

The men at the fort were residents of Indianola before the war. The atmosphere in the dugout is that of a meeting of neighbors with a veneer of military discipline. At thirty, Shea's Irish heritage shows in twinkling blue eyes and a pointed black beard tinged with gray. He believes strongly that repeated participation in a ritual of question and response binds the members of a group into a community despite their divergent motivations. By directing questions to each officer in turn, he makes each response a report to all. He sits down and begins with his usual lead question. "Captain Reuss, what is the health of the battalion?"

Reuss, at thirty-five, has slightly thinning brown hair atop a large head on a short neck. He is a physician and druggist in addition to commanding Company B of the artillery. Looking at his patients, he removes his glasses and replies, "Our health is quite good, Dan. We have one man on sick leave in Indianola with a broken arm. We've had the usual run of cuts and sprains from the bridge building over the bayou to Saluria, but we have no one in hospital here at the fort. There are two men in the small hospital in Saluria recovering from yellow fever."

"And our water supply?"

"Water is marginal at about fifteen days, but it's winter, and we should have rain frequently. Our canvas catchments are in good repair, as are both the wood and concrete cisterns. If we get down to five days' supply, we can send a wagon over to Saluria for a couple hogsheads of water. The town is mostly empty because of the war, and there should be plenty."

Shea has a deep respect for Reuss. His medical training in Germany appears to place him somewhat in advance of his American colleagues. Shea sees him as a good, intelligent man who seems unflappable. He has the quiet self-respect to speak his mind. Shea says, "Thank you, John. Otto Schnaubert has given me a brief report on his examination of the Union ship after our engagement today. I'd like him to give us an expanded version now. As you know, we put three shots into that ship, and I compliment you on excellent gunnery despite the small amount of live-firing practice we've had owing to the shortage of ammunition."

Otto is Reuss's first lieutenant and, at twenty-eight, the second-youngest man among the senior officers. He wants to put his best face forward. He briefly rehearsed his response, anticipating this question. Relating the points of his earlier message, he adds, "It's my estimate she will complete repairs within twenty-four hours and remain on station until replaced. Will Moore tells me the vessel was well handled during the engagement and intentionally approached the fort on that last tack? It's a guess as to their intentions, but they may have been testing our ability to shoot, number of guns, and our range."

The mention of Moore is partly to credit one of his men and partly to give substance to his report. Moore is well liked and generally seen as a bright young man on the way up.

Shea recognizes Otto's military experience, which exceeds that of any other officer in the fort. In managing his battery, he is assertive and confident; but with the other officers, he seems withdrawn, except with Reuss. Shea picks up the conversation.

"It would be easy to say that we accomplished little in shelling that ship. I say we accomplished two important things. First, we can shoot effectively. Union ship captains will not miss that point, and they will stay well offshore. Second, when they are well offshore, they won't be able to shoot over us into the bay and hit the small coasting ships that are now the backbone of our traffic. That's an important accomplishment, as it's our only way to get guns and ammunition into Texas. I see a job well done. Captain Bletchley, do you have anything to report on your infantry?"

"The infantry are in fine shape, Captain. We are ready to protect you if the Union infantry attacks from down the island or from the shore."

Bletchley bears a surprising resemblance to the figure of John Bull that appears in newspaper sketches. He has a round head and face, small eyes, and a beginning pot belly. The Irishman in Shea sees no good in the English Bletchley, whose plantation manners he finds deeply offensive. With his feelings tightly under control, Shea replies only, "Thank you, John, we feel safer now."

Bletchley smiles proudly, missing the subtle sarcasm. The other officers smile slyly, not missing the nuances of Shea's comment.

"Captain Vernon, what is the state of our stores?'

Vernon is also a planter, but Shea finds him agreeable for an Englishman. He tries to foster the community of officers that Shea values. At thirty-five, Vernon commands an artillery company in addition to his responsibilities for supplies. He has a bushy head of very black hair and a monstrous mustache to match. In contrast, his chin is clean shaven. He says simply, "We fired twelve solid shots today. We still have almost two hundred solids and plenty of shrapnel and canister. The supply of powder is adequate."

"And rations?"

"There are fifteen days rations of corn, meal, and beans. The supply boat *Breaker* is expected in a week. Some flatboats will be in from independent farmers with greens and sweet potatoes every few days. The fish are still biting in the bay, and the crabs are waiting in the bayous. We are in good shape, sir."

Shea finds Vernon a reliable officer with a welcome sense of humor among this group of taciturn Germans. He replies, "Very good, John. Do any of you have anything to add?" There is no response, so he continues, "Post the usual lookouts. Double them at the lighthouse with one looking inland and one to seaward. Move one of the twelve-pounders down to cover the bridges to the mainland tonight. Captain Bletchley, please send a platoon of infantry down as pickets for that gun. Move the other twelve-pounder forward to the rifle pits with the other infantry pickets down the island. This run-in with the sloop may be exactly what it appears to be, but it is a change in their tactics to come that close inshore. Changes in tactics on the part of our enemy always make me nervous. I'll see you gentlemen at mess."

Chapter Two

December 7, 1861, 6:00 p.m.

The fort has separate messes for senior and junior officers. The senior officers comprise the fort commander, his three company commanders, and their first lieutenants, all but one married and most with at least one child. In contrast, the junior officers' mess has twelve second lieutenants who are nearly all bachelors below the age of twenty-two. The difference became evident when the junior officers threw a party for the "young ladies" of Indianola that included a moonlight sail and a champagne dinner. The reporter for the newspaper that covered the event would normally be careful to name the "ladies" and give their families bragging rights. But this time, he tactfully failed to name any "young ladies," a telling omission in a small town.

By the winter of 1861-62, the blockade is limiting the foodstuffs available in the coastal region of Texas. Coffee, normally imported from Mexico, is nonexistent. The absence of coffee leads to parched corn or "corn coffee," which is a sorry substitute. Walking to the mess, Reuss thinks about corn coffee and hopes that it would not be served tonight. Shea took pride in his mess, and it would be unkind to refuse it if offered. Reuss chuckles and puts a question to his companion. "Otto, if Shea serves corn coffee tonight, will you drink it?"

Otto, seeing where this might lead, replies, "I would not offend a good man." Reuss considers that an appropriate spirit.

Although coffee is dear, beef is cheap, but lean and tough. Large ranching operations continue to drive cattle to Indianola to be slaughtered for their hides. The blockade of shipping causes the stock of hides to pile up, but hides keep. With no refrigeration, the beef carcasses do not keep and are fed to the hogs or simply abandoned to rot on the prairie. Drivers reclaim a few dollars by butchering and selling the better cuts, even at three pennies a pound.

Otto, continuing his walk to the mess with Reuss, puzzles about a contradiction. He broaches the subject to Reuss. "The plantation operators, so despicable to us Germans for their slavery holdings, are nevertheless the source of food we consume here at the fort. The plantations lost revenue when cotton exports dropped. They've offset that by planting sweet potatoes, corn, beans, and 'greens.' These go directly to the state to be issued as rations or on flatboats down the Lavaca River for sale in Indianola or here at Fort Washington." Reuss grunts, and Otto continues, "As militia, we aren't paid, and with the blockade killing all the jobs, we have no way to make money. That means if it weren't for our rations, we'd have no way to feed our families. As officers, we draw rations for three persons and send two of them home for the wife and kids. That's my problem. I despise their slavery, but without it, I could not feed my family."

"And I suppose, Otto, that you especially hate the idea that those extra rations for officers were supposed to take care of their slave servants. And being the high-minded German that you are, you can't stand it that you are feeding Mary and your daughter off of rations aimed at the slavery that you despise so much."

"Sometimes, Reuss, you see things too clearly."

"Otto, a word of advice: you recall the German saying that if you like sausage, you should never watch it being made. War and politics are that way too."

* * *

Shea sits at the mess with his senior officers, smiles confidently, and starts the conversation with a challenging question. "Gentlemen, the engagement today has caused me to wonder about the utility of the lighthouse. Is it of more value to the Union ships or to us? What's your view?"

That question seems to come as a surprise and elicits a brief silence until Captain Vernon, dabbing his mustache with a napkin, ventures, "Obviously, it has value to us as a lookout point, but that has to be weighed against the value to the Union as a marker for our fort. The fort's highest point is only ten feet above sea level. In short, we are not very visible from seaward. But the lighthouse marks our location all too accurately."

Shea thinks briefly that he can always count on Vernon to lead off in a discussion. He would probably become the commander of the fort if Shea were promoted. Shea's ambition makes this a prime consideration. He glances down at his plate and the mismatched silverware, which speaks the orphan status of a fort manned entirely by militia. Raising his head, he looks questioningly at Bletchley, who says,

"You should not consider just the view to seaward. The lighthouse forms a lookout for any infantry attack from the mainland or from farther down the island. It is an excellent location to direct artillery fire in support of my troops."

Shea nods. He resents being told what he "should not" do but admits to himself that Bletchley has a point.

Reuss says thoughtfully, "Since the lens and light have already been removed and stored ashore, the structure has no military value to the Union at night. It's made of cast iron, and its dark color makes it nearly invisible after sunset. On the other hand, if there is a moon out, we could likely see any Union ships within two or three miles of shore."

Shea thinks for a moment. Reuss always seems to see both sides of a problem. Then he asks, "Otto, what do you think?"

Otto decides this is the opening for an idea that has been in the back of his mind for several weeks. He ventures, "I have a surveying transit, which we could mount on the lighthouse and use as a range finder to the ships. I recovered it from the Union camp at Green Lake when they abandoned their equipment to board ships and go north. At the time, I thought it might be useful in laying out any additions to the fort."

Shea is never sure what he will hear from Schnaubert, and this is a typically novel idea. "Otto, you don't need to defend your capture of Union equipment. How accurately could you determine range?"

"I've worked that out. If we can correct for tide, we could range more accurately than we can point the guns—but if there is any wave action that would degrade the accuracy a little."

Shea sits a moment in silence. The lighthouse question more complicated than he thought. He asks, "Beyer, what's your view?"

Beyer is Vernon's first lieutenant and, at twenty-one, the youngest officer in the mess. He replies, "I won't argue with Otto's math. He's a surveyor, educated at a good German university. But I worry about actually doing this range finding in the middle of an action. The man operating the transit must be well trained and experienced in adjusting the elevation knob. He will have to shout out the reading to another man on the ground, and that man will have to relay it by more shouting, maybe three men, to get the reading to us at the fort. Then Otto will have to correct for the tide level and look up the range on a table. It seems complicated to me. Anyway, we will have the range accurately after the first round by spotting the fall of the shot."

Shea feels that he can always count on Beyer for the practical view of a plan and the self-confidence to speak his mind. He thinks Beyer is probably right. But he will not dampen Otto's enthusiasm for new ideas, saying, "Thank you, gentlemen, you have given me much to think on. Now let's try this fried beef and sweet potatoes."

* * *

The attitude toward the war varies among the population groups of Texas. The plantation owners, mainly of English descent, see the war as a defense of slavery and a preservation of their way of life. A world without plantation aristocracy is unthinkable to them, even on the Texas frontier.

The German settlers of Indianola view slavery as a crime against humanity. They arrived in the 1850s after a widespread war among the various kingdoms and principalities of Germany. In that war, men were conscripted from one part of Germany to fight and kill those in another part of Germany. Abridgement of freedom and "home" produced a large immigration to America. With an antislavery view, these *Auswanderers* initially opposed secession, but the naval blockade soon led them to view the Union as a hated central government, controlling their lives and threatening their homes.

Captain Bletchley says, "The beef and potatoes are very good," then looking at Otto, asks, "Is your wife eating this well?" The German's face turns a deep red, but he says nothing. The implication that he cannot support his family is too near the truth. Looking at the others, Bletchley continues, "Thanks to our plantation and slaves, my family is eating at least this well. Maybe if Indianola had a few slaves, it would help matters. I thank God we are fighting to preserve slavery."

To Otto, this is a double insult. The devil is telling him that his hungry family would benefit if he would just embrace slavery. He fumes and looks down at his plate but holds his tongue. Under the table, his fist clenches. Bletchley is a senior officer, and it would only upset the unity of this group to start a verbal fight in the mess.

Shea clears his throat. The laugh lines at the corners of his eyes disappear as he says, "Mr. Bletchley, I prize the freedom of my officers to speak their views in this mess, but I must remind you that one topic is strictly forbidden. We will *not* talk about *why* we are fighting this war. It should be clear from today's action that we *are* fighting quite effectively and in a united fashion. There are strong differences at this table on the matter of *why* we are fighting. Nothing will be settled and much will be disturbed by plowing that ground. You are free to have your opinions, but I will not suffer your introduction of that topic again."

Bletchley blushes, replying defensively, "I'm just saying how things are at home." But his red face matches Otto's, whose ice-blue eyes fix him steadily across the table.

Vernon, seeing both sides of this conflict, ventures a new topic, inquiring of progress on the bridges over the bayous to the tiny town of Saluria, where a ferry connects with the mainland. The red slowly passes from Otto's face as he stops slashing at the beef on his plate and replies, "We have repaired the first bridge from Matagorda Island. It will now take the load of the twenty-four-pounders and could probably handle thirty-two-pounders if we had them. The second bridge that joins the little island to the wharf at Saluria will be finished in five days."

Vernon continues, "How about the ferry from Saluria to the mainland?"

Otto breaks a wedge of corn bread before replying, "The ferry is adequate to handle one gun, but there is not room for the mules on the same trip. That means we must send a mule team over first to be able to get the gun off when the ferry lands at the main shore. I sincerely hope we never have to evacuate this fort. It would be a terribly slow and complicated maneuver."

Shea says, "We all fervently hope we do not have to evacuate this fort, but it is a matter we have to plan. Now, perhaps, gentlemen, we can make a start on this lovely pecan pie. We can be thankful that the blockade cannot stop production of sugarcane and molasses, and who could imagine Texas without pecans?" A dutiful chuckle went round the table.

* * *

The pie lives up to expectations, and when it is consumed, the men move to their individual quarters in quiet conversation. Reuss and Otto walk together toward a tent they share. The pie has not eased the tension in Otto's stomach, but Reuss seems satisfied, saying, "Don't let him get your dander up. That was a crude thing for him to say. Even Vernon was upset with him. I think you did a good job in holding your temper. You know, I'm never sure whether he is trying to make trouble or just too insensitive to know what he's saying. Either way, he's an ass, but he's Shea's problem, not ours. What about it? You ready to turn in?"

Otto says he wants to check the battery and walks over to the gun ports. Leaning on a gun, he looks seaward. In the light of a half moon, he can just see the masts of the Union sloop. It would be a beautiful view if only the hated ship were not there.

Today, he has likely killed, certainly wounded, several men on that ship—of itself, that is, not new. In four years with the U.S. Artillery, he has killed many men in the third Seminole War and the Comanche Wars in west Texas. But this is different. Those men were defending their homes against a force that would take their lands and end their way of life. The men in the sloop are trying to end his way of life and damage his new home. In the U.S. Artillery, he served the hated role of a central government, killing people in their home lands. Now he is on the other side, defending his land against a central government force. Indeed he thinks this feels better, not good, just better.

CHAPTER THREE

December 8, 1861

Rain fell steadily, blown by occasional wind gusts into a drumbeat on the tent where Reuss and Otto sit on their cots, smoking in thoughtful silence. The odors of wet canvas and pipe smoke permeate the enclosed tent. The Meerschaum pipe that Otto holds is a gift from his father, which is carefully preserved and enjoyed for the seven years since he left Germany. He carefully strokes the warm bowl of the pipe, and his thoughts are on the family home in southern Saxony. He pictures the magnificent Erzgebirge Mountains and the small lakes so different from the flat treeless land of the Texas coast. Yet this new treeless land is now home to his beginning family. It may not have beauty, but it has energy and promise. It will grow to be a major shipping hub, and he would be part of it as a surveyor and civil engineer.

His thoughts are brought back to the chilly tent when Reuss speaks, "We're meeting with Shea this morning. He wants to move the guns to a new location. Your comment the other evening about the transit prompted him to propose that you be assigned to do some mapping and layout for a new fortification. I know surveying is your second love after Mary, so I gladly said yes."

The smile spreads quickly across Otto's face as he asks, "Shall we leave now?" In a moment, he is dressed against the rain and ready to leave. Reuss laughs to himself as they duck under the tent flap for the short walk to the headquarters.

*   *   *

At the dugout, the two men shake rain off their rubberized ponchos, lay them aside, and walk to the table where Shea sits facing a pile of papers. "Gentlemen," he says, pushing forward a chair and clearing it of a worn map case, "take a seat and let's discuss an idea I have about protecting Pass Cavallo." Both men settle into camp chairs and wait for Shea to continue.

His brow furrows as he glances down at the map on his desk. Looking up, he begins, "As you know, our present location is completely exposed to the guns of any Union ship in the Gulf. We have been fortunate so far because the guns on the blockading ships could not outrange ours. But the day will come when some ship with a rifled sixty-four-pounder will stand out of the range of our guns and blast us to pieces. Equally as bad, we are open to attack on our flank and in the rear by any Union land force that can come up from the other end of the island. That would block our path of retreat, and we would be overcome."

He pauses as if considering what all of this implied for their future prospects then, pointing with his hand, says, "The actual Pass Cavallo is a mile and a half north of us, where the width narrows to maybe two hundred yards. If we could place the guns at that narrow neck, we could cover the pass at close range. Also, the Union ships approaching the pass would be heading straight toward our guns and unable to bring their main guns to bear. Further, we would be close to a line of retreat over the bridges to Saluria. We could be protected from land attack by a simple line of trenches encircling us and anchored on the bayou. What do you think?"

Reuss nods and says, "You know my opinion, Dan, I'm all for it."

Shea's questioning gaze shifts to Otto, who takes the cue. "Major Shea, I think the idea is excellent. As I've said, our retreat from here would be tedious and time consuming. There is a little more elevation at the place you propose so that we could have a good bombproof dugout for the troops."

Shea, relaxing, leans back in his chair and asks, "What are the problems?"

"Excavations for the fort and the trenches would not be a problem, but we have no source of wood for structures and supports. There's not a tree on the whole island. A lot of timber would have to be brought in on supply boats. But despite that, I think it's an excellent idea."

The magnitude of this aspect had not occurred to Shea. He pauses then says, "How much timber would be needed?"

"I can't say off hand, but I'd like to look over the ground and give you an estimate in two days."

Shea, leaning forward, elbows on the table, smiles, and says, "Otto, I want you to do more than that. Could you take that transit you captured from the Yankees and make me an accurate map of the area, including the pass and showing the elevations and the layout for the guns and a bombproof shelter?"

Otto, sitting on the edge of his chair, smiled. He would get to do some surveying and a break from the routine of camp life. He might even get a reputation as a civil engineer that could mean employment after the war. The world brightens. "I'd like that very much, but I'll need a rodman and a chainman, with Captain Reuss's permission? I think we could have your map in about four days."

Shea strokes his pointed beard. This is working out just as he hoped. "Excellent, we're having a visit by an engineering colonel from Galveston in five days. That gives me a chance to review the map with you and be ready to put the matter to him in a timely fashion. You and Reuss decide on the men you need and get started right away."

* * *

Back in their tent, the two men discuss the choices of surveying assistants. Otto says, "As far as I know, none of our men have surveying experience. I'll need someone who learns quickly and follows directions rigorously. I'd like to have John Noll, Mary's father. He's very intelligent, and we already know each other well. He would make a good rodman. The choice for chainman is less critical but needs someone in good physical condition. My first choice would be George Eberhart, but there could certainly be others."

Reuss thinks on that and comments, "I know John is getting tired of being a sergeant. This might be a good change for him. For the chainman, how about my son-in-law George Rochow?" Otto approves. Reuss continues, "Meet with them and get started. I'll ask George French to fill in for you while you're on this chore. And, Otto, do a good job of it. I'm tired of being hung out here in front of the whole Union navy like Mollie's drawers on a clothesline."

* * *

Walking over to the battery, Otto locates John Noll and asks his view on the project. As Shea had guessed, he is eager to stop being a sergeant for a few days and learn a new trade. George Rochow is not quite so enthusiastic but still curious about what a chainman does and welcomes a break from routine. The three of them walk over to the tent to unpack and examine the surveying equipment.

The rain slows down, allowing a weak sunlight to illuminate the tent in step with the men's rising spirit of adventure. Otto lifts the brass transit from its mahogany box and marvels at the beauty of its mechanisms. He says, "This transit measures the elevation angle of an object viewed through its little telescope. It also indicates the compass bearing of the sight line to that object." He carefully avoids the mathematics involved in using these numbers, as the men will not have to do the calculations. Not everyone thinks that math is beautiful.

He unwraps the rod and says, "John, you place this pointed brass foot on a reference point, and then I will signal you to move the red and white target up or down the length of the rod. When the target is aligned with the crosshairs in the transit's telescope, the target indicates the difference in height between its reference point and that of the transit. I'd like for you to handle that, but you'll have to be patient, as it takes time to get it all right."

John leans back from his examination of the rod. "Otto, it all sounds straightforward. I'm for it as a break from camp life. Who knows, maybe we can start a family surveying business when this war is over."

Unpacking the heavy chain, Otto hands it to Rochow, saying, "George, this is simply a very long tape measure that will find the distance between the rod and the transit. It's heavy, and the chainman always seems to walk further carrying it than the rest of the crew with their instruments. What do you think?"

George, his strength challenged, lifts the chain easily. I'm with John—it would be a great break from camp routine and maybe a new trade after the war. It's not as heavy as it looks."

* * *

When all the questions were answered, the new survey crew steps out to try its first measurements. John gets a wagon and mule to carry the equipment to the new site, saying, "I got Maggie—she's a big strong mule and will handle a lightly loaded wagon all by herself." She was not hard to find, being at least a hand taller than average and with a "heads up" stance that raised her ears even higher above the pack.

Loading their equipment, they drive to the point where Shea wishes to set the guns. Otto feels a little tired but tells himself that it's just the excitement. He produces a three-foot length of wood sharpened at one end and, using a heavy mallet, drives it into the sand until only six inches protrude. He marks an X on the top of the stake with a pen knife. This would be the basic data point for the survey. The tripod is set over the stake and the transit secured on top.

The transit is a marvelous precision machine to Otto, revealing the dedicated craftsmanship that produced it. This transit, made by the German firm of Keuffel and Esser, spoke to him of all that the good technology of his native country. He gently strokes it with a scrap of flannel to remove any moisture before he adjusts the leveling screws.

* * *

An hour and a half later, they completed the data to measure the distance from the near shore and to the opposite side of Pass Cavallo marked by Pelican Island. The men perform well with the attention and patience necessary for accurate readings, but Otto is thoroughly exhausted.

They drive back to the fort. Maggie thinks that a little three-mile trip with a lightly loaded wagon is the way that mules should live and turns eagerly for the trip home.

Both Noll and Rochow are intrigued with their new task and the possibility of learning a different trade. They soon became the center of conversation as they tell of a new fortification. Rumor enlarges upon this, and the size of the new fort grows twofold by nightfall. Neither man is about to correct this, for as the fort grows in story, their importance in its planning grows also. Altogether, it is a good arrangement.

* * *

Getting to his tent, Otto knows what is coming in his physical problem. When serving in Florida, he contracted malaria, and the symptoms recur from time to time. He takes off his uniform and, in his long johns underwear, wraps himself in blankets, and lies down on his cot.

Reuss finds him there a half hour later, shivering, teeth clenched, and his hair wringing wet with sweat. Reuss has been Otto's doctor for two years and knew his medical history well. He challenges, "Have you forgotten to take your quinine?"

The shaking is modified momentarily with a nod of the head. Pawing through a box under his cot, Reuss finds a bottle of powder. Filling a bowl with water from his canteen and taking a healthy pinch of the quinine, he says, "Open up, Otto, and don't bite my finger." Placing the powder on Otto's tongue and offering the water to eliminate the horrid taste, he administers the dose quickly. Otto continues his violent shaking from the deep chills racking his body. Reuss resumes, "I'm going to put you in hospital tomorrow morning if this doesn't improve tonight."

Otto's hopes fade. Just when he is about to get some recognition as a surveyor, he throws it all away by forgetting his medicine. He feels sorry for himself for an hour then sternly commands that he get over this damn shaking. The command is ineffective. Reuss prepares an oral dose of laudanum. It's administered by holding Otto's nose closed until his mouth opens and then releasing the nose and pouring the draft into his mouth. After a while, the tremors subside, and he falls asleep.

* * *

The sun is up when Reuss says, "Otto, get out of that wet underwear. Here's a washcloth to scrub yourself and a dry suit of underwear to get into. We'll go down to breakfast and see if you can give an imitation of a reasonably fit soldier. If you can't, it will be the hospital. If you can, Shea doesn't need to know about this."

Otto does as he is told and feeling weak, but at least over the chills, they set off for the mess. He fortifies the "corn coffee" with an extra load of sugar, and at least it felt hot despite the burned taste. The cornmeal mush was also hot, and after a bowl, it seems that he might survive the day. Reuss notes the slight change in color and is willing to forego hospitalization.

Shea asking, "How does the mapmaking go?" receives the reply that the crew worked well and that the sights were taken for the pass. Today's work will concentrate on measurements of the bridges and elevation lines for the fort area. Shea seems pleased. Otto feels that he has passed a school exam.

* * *

Back at the tent, Otto says, "We fooled Shea all right." Reuss snorts and replies, "You don't give him enough credit. He saw right through both of us as soon as he spotted your white face and shaky hands. He has a problem, you know. He wants this new fort to be recognized as his idea. If you make the drawing, that will happen. But if you don't, then Colonel Garland will make the drawing, and the fort will be Garland's idea. Our commander is a good judge of men and a damn good soldier, but he's also ambitious. Promotion is his goal, and killing the enemy is one way to get there. Killing the enemy and having smart ideas is quicker. You are the only one that can produce Shea's drawing. He does not want to kill you with work, but he needs that drawing."

Otto thinks that the fort has more than one good judge of men. Reuss adds, "Otto, quit today when you start to feel tired, tell the men whatever you want, but get back here, take your medicine, and get in bed. If you kill yourself, there will be some sad people—Mary will have to raise that baby by herself, Shea won't have his drawing, and I will have killed my patient."

* * *

Otto calls an end to the work shortly after noon. Maggie feels this is the way for mules to work—four hours a day with an unloaded wagon and extra grain in a nose bag. She turns briskly for home, where she can raise her head above the poor ordinary mules.

And so it goes until on the fourth day. Otto's handshakes are reduced, allowing him to put the legends on the drawing with only minor wiggles in the letters. The pass proves to be only 204 yards wide. The path of a ship forcing the pass would be very predictable and only four hundred yards from the gun position. In his tent, he studies the drawing and can see himself laying the guns to strike the ship. The creative engineer of his early training is replaced in his thoughts by the destructive warrior of his later experience. He hardly notices the transition.

Chapter Four

December 12, 1861

Reuss and Otto again sit at the table with Shea who is clearly in excellent spirits. He says, "Your map work and surveys did the trick. Colonel R. R. Garland has reviewed the entire scheme. He complimented your work, Otto. Let me read from the report he will send to the adjutant general in Galveston."

> *The point selected by Major Shea to establish his battery is, in my opinion, the proper position to command the entrance to the bay and, if properly constructed under the supervision of an experienced engineer officer and suitably appointed, could be made to accomplish the object. But in its present condition, it is totally inadequate for this purpose and should be immediately withdrawn or put in a condition not only to command the pass but to be capable of defending itself from attack by sea or land.*

"I compliment you both. Now, since this report must be delivered to Indianola, I thought that Otto might serve as messenger." Turning to Otto, he says, "I've written a seventy-two-hour pass that should allow you to complete the assignment and briefly enjoy the comforts of home. There's also a saddlebag of letters from the officers and men that you could deliver to the post office or, if you wish, directly to their homes."

* * *

Otto dresses in his best outfit, saddles and mounts a mule, and rides for Saluria. The mule is lightly loaded with the two saddlebags of mail and the large bags of supplies that he is taking to Mary. It stands quietly on the ferry, which moves slowly across the channel to the main shore. It is frightened by the crosspieces on the ramp that the ferry let down on the shore. Then with a jacket over its head and some strong urging, it steps onto the ramp, slips then recovers, and finds the shore, which stands solid under its feet. Now mule and rider are on the road to Indianola, and the sounds of birds, sights, and smells of scattered flowers are familiar and comforting to both the mule and rider.

The mule knows the way to Indianola and maintains a steady walk. In the warm sunshine, Otto, lulled by the soft thumps of the mule's shoes on the road and the steady groans of the leather saddle, relaxes into thoughts of Mary.

1857

He first met her by a fortunate accident. His artillery company moved by ship from Florida to Texas on their way to the New Mexico Indian Wars. Men and guns on separate ships did not arrive together, requiring a two-day layover in Indianola. One of those days was Sunday. He found a Methodist church and entered for the service. Seated across the aisle and a row in front sat the most striking young teenage girl he had ever seen. She had gleaming black hair and blue eyes, which looked like they wanted to smile but did not dare in that holy place.

After the sermon, the minister moved to greet his flock individually at the exit. When Otto appeared, he said, "Young man, are you a long way from home?"

Otto, dressed in his best blue U.S. Army uniform, answered, "Yes, sir, I was born in Württemberg." It was the first thing that came into his head, but it brought a huge smile to the minister's face.

"There's someone I want you to meet." Motioning with his hand, he beckoned forward a large man, dutifully followed by the stunning girl. When they approached, he said, "You two have a common background—you're both from Württemberg. Maybe you could discuss old times on the church lawn while I finish greeting my people."

Both of the *Württembergers* looked a little puzzled. The larger, older man took the initiative and said, "I'm John Noll. My family is from Heilbronn in the state of Württemberg."

This brought a big smile to Otto's face, and he replied, "I'm Otto Schnaubert. I was born in the city of Württemberg, but I know your family name. I believe you were farmers in Heilbronn."

It turned out that John Noll recognized the Schnaubert name as a professor at the University of Chemnitz. Otto allowed that was his uncle and that Otto had studied *Landwirtschaft,* or surveying, at the university. This broke the formal European ice, and John presented Mary Noll, who now blushed slightly and tried, with little success, to look demure. The minister appeared, saying, "John, if my information is right, this young man will be here just for a day or two. Perhaps you could show him the hospitality of our city over dinner while you talk about old times in Württemberg."

John saw that his daughter could hardly wait for him to say yes, and after all, the young man was educated. If he would only be here for a day, nothing much could come of it. So he said, "Why don't we all go home and see what your mother has on the table? I think we could feed another mouth."

* * *

In good German housewifely style, the mother had prepared a Sunday dinner that would support several extra mouths. It did with fried sausage, sauerkraut, and spaetzle followed with peach fritters. Talk turned to "the old country" and its beauty. Otto's fond memories of the beautiful German countryside could not take his attention away from the lovely girl. Then he thought of a promising tactic, saying, "I have done drawing and sketches most of my life,

Mr. Noll. Could I make a sketch of your wife and Mary to repay you for this wonderful dinner?"

John was clever enough to see right through this, but mother and daughter were both flattered and giggled as they cleared dishes. John said, "Yes, I'll find some of Mary's school paper and a pencil." After all, nothing much could come of it.

The sketch turned out wonderfully; everyone expressed their pleasure, and Otto got to look at Mary for the better part of an hour. She proved to be as stunning as she had first appeared. The picture received an honored place on the mantle over the fireplace, and John promised to frame it the next week.

Late in the afternoon, Otto announced that he must return to the ship by five o'clock and stood to make his departure. Mary, who had been silent most of the afternoon, said, "I hear that soldiers look forward to receiving mail from home. Would it be all right if I were to write to you?" This last question directed both to Otto and to her father. John gave it some thought and said with ponderous decision, "I think that would be all right." After all, what could come of it?

1861

The mule snorts, and its step quickens when it detects the odor of alfalfa forage from nearby Indianola. The movement brings Otto back from his dream. He skirts the business section and heads for Old Town, which had become the residential section. Riding to the extreme north edge, he stops at the house Mary occupies and dismounts, yelling, "Hello the house!" When the door opens, with hat in hand, he says, "Madam, could you furnish hospitality for a soldier and a mule?" Mary pauses and, in mock seriousness, says, "It all depends on which one is asking—on second thought, maybe it does not matter. I'm so glad to see you!"

She throws her arms around him without regard for the mud that spatters his clothes and, pulling his head down, plants a huge kiss on his lips. He embraces her, lifting her lightly off the ground, and marvels at this small, lovely woman that he is fortunate enough to call wife. Mary feels breathless with surprise but manages to say, "Put the mule away and come to the kitchen. Lina Katlyn is asleep. I want to hear all about what you have been doing."

He hands her the sacks of supplies, steals another kiss, and leads the mule to the barn behind the house. Later, opening the door to the kitchen, he is greeted by warm air and the sight of two women. Mary says, "Otto, this is Frances Dickerson. She and her mother helped me with Lina Katlyn when she was born. Now after school, we sew together for the troops at the fort."

Otto turns to offer a nod of recognition to a young girl, of perhaps fifteen, not as lovely as Mary but definitely well favored. She is blushing slightly and smiling discreetly as she hurries to gather up sewing with the sure knowledge of her sex that a man and wife who had not seen each other for two months need some time alone. Otto interrupts with "Wait a moment, Frances, I think I have something for you."

Pawing through his saddlebag and finding what he searched for, he says, "Yes, there's a letter from Will Moore addressed to a Miss Frances Dickerson. That must be you." The blush on her face confirms it as she says, "Oh, it's from Will! I must run home and read it. And, Mr. Schnaubert, could you take a letter I have back to him?" Otto nods yes. She grabs her sewing and is out the door quickly with the letter clasped to her bosom.

Mary says with a sigh and a frown, "I am a little worried about her. She is terribly smitten with Will Moore, and she is so young."

"Yes, Mary, she's no older than you were when we first met."

"Oh, don't be ridiculous, I'm going to be twenty next year, and then I'll be an older woman." This last is said with a pained look on her face. He marvels that anyone so lovely, who retained a stunning figure and whose smile warmed the kitchen better than the cookstove, could think of herself as "an older woman."

Pulling up a kitchen chair, he sits, saying, "What's this sewing that you and Frances are up to?"

"We get cloth from the prison at Huntsville and sew uniforms for the militia. I expect some of your men are wearing shirts we have sewn. Did you know the prisoners weave a million yards of cloth per year?"

The question goes unanswered as a muffled cry comes from the bedroom, and Mary says, "Come see your lovely daughter. She will be nine months old next week."

Lina Katlyn lies in a wooden crib mounted on rockers and announces the state of her diapers to the world in general. Otto, in false modesty, steps back to the kitchen as Mary changes the baby. Soon, she returns with a quiet Lina who is looking at the face of this strange man. He tries poking a finger at her. This elicits a big smile and a clumsy grab for the finger. The baby has more hair than he remembers, and the eyes have grown bluer. *Could she possibly grow up to be as beautiful as her mother?*

Mary moves to a comfortable chair in the warm kitchen and starts to nurse the baby. Otto watches with conflicting emotions. Mary's breasts are as lovely as he remembers, but clearly he now had to share them. *Older woman indeed.*

Mary breaks the silence, "She is such a good baby. She sleeps through the night and is never any trouble. Dr. Reuss's wife stopped by last week to look at her and said that she's in good health and growing just fine. It's grand to have neighbors like her and Frances."

Mary completes the nursing and moves Lina back to the cradle. Then she begins to prepare dinner by feeding the stove and getting out a large iron frying pan. A small cry sends her back to the bedroom. When she returns with Lina over her shoulder, Mary is lightly bouncing up and down and patting Lina on the back. Otto concentrates on the bouncing breasts and wonders if Mary knew what that does to a man who had not even seen a woman in two months. A loud burp brings the bouncing to an end, and Mary asks if he would move the cradle into the kitchen. This was done, and Lina's gurgles compete with the sound of frying.

Otto looks at the pan on the stove and sees slabs of cornmeal mush and two slices of bacon. A pot on the back of the stove begins to puff. In a few minutes, Mary serves their plates with the fried mush, bacon, and red beans, the same food as at the fort. She smiles proudly as if this was the world's finest banquet. Then he thinks, *Where else would she get food than the sacks that I bring home on visits?* Bletchley had been all too accurate, but Mary's spirit seems to conquer it all.

He says, "Mary, how's our money holding up? There was not all that much of it when this conflict began."

"I had not told you, but I do some additional sewing beyond that for the troops. It serves to pay the rent, and we are doing nicely. I also sold one of your watercolor paintings, the one of the wharf at Lavaca. You never liked it, but I thought it nice. A woman who had taken art lessons from you three years ago bought it."

Again, conflicting emotions—happy that someone liked his painting, which he did not particularly care for, sad that Mary has to scrimp to pay the rent, and pride that she manages so well in difficult times. Does he really deserve this remarkable woman? Lina's eyes close, and her breathing becomes slow and steady.

Mary says, "Otto, there's a pot of hot water on the stove. Would you like a sponge bath?" This is a luxury. At the fort, there is not enough water for baths, and the alternative is a dip in the Gulf. In wintertime, this requires fortitude, and he thinks with embarrassment how long it had been since he last bathed. While he undresses, Mary fetches a small washtub and empties the pot from the stove. She produces a large sponge and begins the slow process of sponging, while he stands on newspapers spread on the kitchen floor. She does a thorough job, and there is no way he could disguise his rising passion for this woman. Mary smiles subtly, saying, "I see you have brought me something," and disappears into the bedroom.

When Otto has dried himself and walks to the bedroom door, he sees Mary's shining black hair spread on the pillow. A delicate white hand turns back the covers on his side of the bed. He slips between the sheets and gently kisses her, his hand finding her swollen breast.

Older woman indeed. Slowly, carefully, he enters her. *Oh god, this is too much, this is too soon. Oh god*—he explodes! Mary says quietly, "Don't worry, we have all night,"—they did. Lina slept through it all—repeatedly.

Chapter Five

December 13, 1861

Otto awakens to a brilliant, cloudless day. He cannot remember a world so filled with promise. Mary is in the kitchen and has moved Lina and the cradle there with her. He thinks, *How does such a small lady do such heavy work?* With a slight blush, he retrieves his clothes from the kitchen, dresses, and joins Mary. Lina is cooing in her cradle, thoroughly happy with the world, and clasping a carved wooden figure.

Mary, smiling, delivers a bowl of cornmeal mush and a cup of corn coffee trailing the odor of warm molasses. There is even corn bread. Otto, starting on a slice, grins happily, saying, "I wish the cook at camp knew how to make corn bread this good."

Mary turns from the stove. "Erdmuthe, Frances's mother showed me. She makes up for the lack of an egg—they're terribly expensive, you know. She adds more lard then cuts back just a little on the baking powder and adds a little water. I would never have figured that out by myself."

Women, thinks Otto. *They are so supportive, at least the* hausfraus *are.* Shea has to work to get a community of his officers helping each other. The ladies seem to conspire and find that community by themselves. Setting aside this puzzle, he says to Mary, "I've got to go out this morning to deliver letters and see what the town looks like. Maybe it's changed in the last seven months."

"I'll wait to have lunch until you get back. Lina will probably be asleep by then."

* * *

Otto saddles the mule and notices the small "U.S." branded on its rump. *Well*, he thinks, *we have the Yankees to thank for you.* When the Union garrisons of Texas and the New Mexico territory evacuated through Indianola at the start of the war, with shipping in short supply, there was just enough space for the men. Mules, tents, wagons, and stores were simply left behind. All of this was a windfall to the Confederacy. The mule Maggie had been obtained from a local farmer, and her unblemished rump testified that she had never been a Yankee.

Otto first stopped at Reuss's house where his knock is answered by a smiling Mrs. Reuss. Handing her a letter, Otto says, "I want to thank you for all the help you have given to Mary and the baby. It's grand having friends like you and John."

Mrs. Reuss experiences a sharp intake of breath and a rise in spirits as she looks at the envelope, recognizing John's handwriting. Smiling warmly, she says, "You are indeed fortunate, Otto, an absolutely beautiful wife and a healthy baby. Knock on wood."

"John and I talked about your son Augustus. He hopes that after med school, the two of them could practice together."

"Augie is in school now, but you can tell John that his grades look very good. That dream just might come true. He talks a lot about his father and wants to go out on house calls with him when he's back in town."

Otto shuffles the letters and extracts one, saying, "I have one here from Sergeant Rochow for his wife. I believe that's your daughter. Can I leave it with you?"

"She stays here with us now, so that will be convenient. We're just one big family—without men."

Otto talks on for a while then, pleading necessity to deliver mail, takes his leave and, mounting the mule, turns for the business district.

* * *

The first stop is the Confederate army office. The commander is out, but his orderly exchanges letters, taking the bundle from Otto and giving him a bag for the fort. The orderly is more gossipy than he should be. Otto learns that Galveston expects an attack from the Union ships at any time and hears the opinion that the island is not defensible. Otto departs greatly informed, but thinking the orderly has been left alone in the office too often with nothing to do but read the passing mail, a small voice counseled, *That is not your problem.*

The next stop is the post office, where the bulk of the letters are left for delivery to the soldiers' families and a mailbag for the fort picked up.

Having discharged his formal duties, he turns the mule toward the business district. Here, his eyes meet one change after another. First, there is the silence. Where there would normally be a background babble of voices and wagon sounds, it is now so silent that he clearly hears the creak of his stirrup leathers rubbing against the saddle and the light jingle of the metal in the bridle.

There are no men visible in town and only a few women. Otto recalls reading in the *Indianola Bulletin* that the number of enlistments in Texas in 1861 had been greater than the number of voters in any previous year. Most men of voting age must be in service. One look down Water Street confirms it.

He rides to the second wharf, ties up the mule, and sticks his head through the warehouse door. Normally, this room would yield a wonderful aroma of coffee from the sacks of beans piled on the floor. Today, there is just a faint fishy smell from the beach, and the room is empty except for dirt, an empty sack, and a few short lengths of rope.

The hotel next to the main wharf is boarded up, and the restaurant next door is closed. Seeing an acquaintance on the street, Otto stops and, after a greeting, asks, "How long has the hotel been closed?"

The reply is "About three months. When the blockade started, they lost all the passengers that stopped over from the Morgan Line ships. They thought business would come back, but you know how it went. By late August, they gave up."

"And the restaurant?"

"The restaurant depended on the hotel, so when one went, they both went."

Thanking the man, he walks toward the Henry Runge Building. It is a general store in the truest sense of the word, including hardware, food, clothes, and even a bank. Inside, Otto walks slowly, examining merchandise and nodding to, first, one and then another acquaintance.

Food is the first surprise—beef at two cents a pound, but coffee is five dollars a pound, and a lettered card says, "We have no coffee this week." Kidney beans are three cents a pound, while eggs are five dollars per dozen, but the box is empty. The greatest surprise is a cheap gingham dress in a bright red check with a tag, reading "$39.50." He reflects that a private in the Confederate States Army receives $37.50 per month and that would not even buy his wife a cheap dress. *What a crazy war*, he thinks. The Union blockades cotton shipments out of the South, and their New England mills have nothing to work with. Then blockade runners bring cotton at exorbitant prices to the mills, and dresses come out at even more exorbitant prices.

He scowls with a faint upset in his stomach, then a friendly voice says, "Good morning, Otto." He turns and finds Henry Runge extending a welcoming hand.

"Good morning, Mr. Runge. I was just admiring your merchandise. How is your store doing in these difficult times?"

Henry's expression briefly looks as if he tasted something foul then brightens half a notch as he says, "Times are very hard, Otto. We all thank you for the protection you give us with the fort, but the blockade makes things nearly impossible. Take that dress you were looking at. We sold that for $3.50 last year. Now it's more than ten times higher. I argued with myself about even putting it out at that price. It probably won't sell, and even if it does, I'll make almost nothing on it. It will just offend my customers."

Otto asks, "How hard has the blockade been on the town's other businesses?"

Again, Henry scowls and replies, "My store will not go under, but many have closed, and more are barely hanging on. I guess that the town's sales these past six months were less than a third of the same period last year. But you know, Otto, our German determination is what keeps us going, and Indianola is mostly German families. We will come through. When the war is over, the growth of trade will be amazing, and we will all prosper."

Otto says something favorable about German spirit but wonders how much worse this could get. It is time to turn the conversation to a new topic. "Mr. Runge, when do you think work might resume on the railroad spur? I surveyed the right of way when that started. I've surveyed the new fort and hope to do more work after the war."

"You must know that there will be no work until after the war. I would guess that then, the work on a railroad will begin and continue for some time. We are the best connection from the East Coast to the West and California. That will be very important. The war runs on California gold. When this is over, all that gold will be available for investment, and it will come right through here."

They talk on for a short time, and Otto feels better about long-range prospects, even if the short range looks bleak. *How bad will it get before it gets better? How will Mary make it?*

* * *

Returning home, Otto unsaddles the mule, pulls down some forage from the loft, and turns to the house. When he opens the door, wonderful aromas fill his nostrils. Mary says, "You're just in time," and, wrapping her hands in a towel, takes a beef roast from the oven. Lina laughs noisily and waves a wooden carving in the air. There are two potatoes alongside the roast along with a couple of carrots. Mary smiles wickedly and says, "While you were gone, I picked up some food to restore your strength."

Otto thinks that might be a first-class idea. Thirty minutes later, with his belly full, he feels the need for a short nap, which he allows just "to restore my strength." It did as he proved later that evening.

* * *

The next morning, the mule is saddled, and Otto gives Mary a huge hug and kiss before returning to the fort. Noticing tears at the corners of Mary's eyes, he turns in the saddle, saying, "If anyone at the fort asks, I'll have to say I had the time of my life in Indianola."

Mary, pouting, says, "Don't you do any such thing, you'll ruin my reputation, I'm just a simple *hausfrau*."

"You fooled me," says Otto, "I thought you were an older woman." The mule moves off quickly, avoiding a slash from Mary's dish towel.

* * *

When the mule steps ashore from the ferry, it knows from sight and smell that home is near and in the direction it is heading. The pace increases. Otto is astounded to see that work has already started on the new fort. Construction crews can be seen digging the trenches for the new location. Surprisingly, Bletchley can be seen supervising construction of the trenches. His stomach knots. This is his job. Bletchley had nothing to do with its design, yet there he is lording himself atop a hill of sand. With teeth clenched, Otto hurries to the dugout to deliver the letters and learn if he will have a role in construction of the new fort.

Chapter Six

December 24, 1861

Otto rides to the rope picket line for the mules at Fort Washington and dismounts. Walking to the headquarters dugout, his anguish builds at the duplicity of Shea, who turned the construction job over to Bletchley after sending Otto on an errand to Indianola. Giving the mailbag to the orderly, he strides up to the desk that Shea normally uses. There he finds two officers, Shea and a colonel whose name is known to him by reputation. Shea says, "Otto, Colonel Garland will be the engineering officer-in-charge of the work at the new fort."

Garland, slightly balding and definitely senior to anyone at the fort, indicates a chair, saying, "Please sit down, Lieutenant. I've been over your drawings for the new fortification and must compliment you on a thorough and accurate job. Captain Bletchley volunteered the use of his own slaves in construction work, and I've put him in charge of digging the trenches and excavating the bombproof dugout. The slaves are accustomed to his direction. That should work out best."

Rearranging himself in the chair, Garland unrolls Otto's drawing of the new fort. Pointing to a line on the drawing, he says, "I have added something to your plan. There should be a mule-drawn railway from the beach up to the dugout to permit easy unloading of supplies and heavy goods that will be brought in by small boats."

Otto sees a crosshatched line about five hundred feet in length with the notation "standard rail spacing." Garland continues, "I understand that you did surveying for the railroad embankment at Indianola." Otto nods. He is unsure where this might lead, but his hopes rise that maybe he will have a role as an engineer in the new fort's construction.

"Good," says Garland. "I want you to take charge of the survey and construction of the railway. That requires more skill than digging ditches. I have indicated a rise of one foot per one hundred feet in length. That should permit a single mule to move loads of up to six thousand pounds. That way, if we have some very heavy ordnance to bring in, we can readily move it up to the fort."

Shea says, "You can take as many as fifty men from your company to do the work. I have already talked that over with Reuss."

"Where will we get the material?" Otto asks.

Shea nods, saying, "You know the ties and rails that are stacked up in Indianola, waiting for the construction of the spur to Victoria? We will pay the railway for what we need. They won't start their construction until after the war." Handing over a paper, he continued, "Here, I have signed a requisition for 1,200 feet of rail and five hundred ties and all the connections, spikes, and tools. Also, I have commissioned a schooner to load and transport that material to the beach at the new location. It will be at the wharf in Saluria day after tomorrow in the morning. I'd like you to go on board and see that the loading and off-loading goes smoothly. Any questions?" Otto had none. He folds the requisition and puts it into his jacket pocket. Rising, he asks, "Anything further?" There is none.

* * *

Otto walks briskly out of the dugout, looking for John Noll. His search at Fort Washington is not successful, so he mounts the mule and rides to the new fort. He sees John sitting atop a sand dune, watching the slaves dig trenches in the sand. Dismounting, he asks, "Are you learning anything?"

"I'm learning more than I want to know." He tries unsuccessfully to wipe the scowl off his face and continues, "He treats those slaves worse than animals." Otto turns to look in the direction John is facing and sees Bletchley atop a dune with a stout switch in his hand, yelling at one of the workers.

"Look at that one's back." The men are working without shirts, and Otto can clearly see the scars across the man's shoulders. His anger rises at the cruel act of slavery made even worse by that kind of treatment. Knowing he can do nothing about it, his frustration rises. After a moment, he orders himself to calm down.

Striving to change the topic, he says to John, "Come on, I want to show you our new job." He leads the mule, and John walks with him until they reach the location for the new railway. Otto says, "Mary is in great good health, and so is your granddaughter. She is going to be a beauty like her mother. Mary sends her love to you and hopes you will have a chance to visit soon." John's scowl slowly turns to a smile as his thoughts shift away from Bletchley and over to his happiness as a father and grandfather. The world looks brighter.

Arriving at the beach, Otto points up the slope, saying, "We are going to survey and build a mule-powered railway from here up to the new fort. We will take off tomorrow for Christmas and then start loading rails and ties the next day at the wharf in Indianola. We can use fifty men from our company to do the track work. The surveying should not take more than half a day. I'd like you, Will Moore, and George Rochow to come with me on the schooner day after tomorrow. Will and George can help with the loading, and maybe you could spend a few hours with your family." John's broad smile indicates complete agreement. He says simply, "I'm ready to go."

* * *

The small fort does what it can to celebrate Christmas Day with the limited range of food stores the state provides. Creativity will depend on what is available locally. The men carefully comb through the sand backstop at the fort's rifle range and gather the lead balls buried there. These are not usable but can be beaten flat against a rock and then cut into small pieces to make bird shot. The smoothbore muskets serve moderately well as shotguns. The result is that roast bird will be served in all of the mess halls.

Reuss's company, through skill or luck, has eight Canadian geese. The senior officers' mess has three canvasback ducks. Even the least fortunate platoon has four mallards. These were supplemented with a mound of sweet potatoes and a pot of rice and red beans.

Vernon's company puts their effort into fishing and boasts a mound of boiled blue crab and several baked redfish. They coast both sides of the island—the bay side, where the crabs lived, and the Gulf side, where the redfish swam.

The senior officers' mess sends a flatboat over to Palacios for oysters, some of which it shares with the junior officers. In exchange, the junior officers send two bottles of champagne from Lt. Christian French's liquor store in Indianola.

*   *   *

Shea sits at the head of the senior officers' mess table and scans the walls of the room. They are lined with boards, which were the siding of houses in Saluria the Yankees had demolished during a raid. He thought of the waste but also the recovery by his troops in creating a useful room, carefully sorting and nailing the boards to the heavy timber supports. What a contrast! Champagne, in a room made of trash wood, bubbles on his tongue and a faint fall of sand from the dugout's roof.

It is a gala occasion for all in a bleak and solitary isolation. Late in the night, the soft tones of "Tannenbaum, O Tannenbaum" come from a group of carolers in Reuss's company area.

*   *   *

The following day, Otto, John Noll, George Rochow, and Will Moore stand on the dock at Saluria and survey the small schooner *Breaker*. Shea has commissioned it to haul railway material. The ship's captain waits with his crew of two on board the tiny vessel. Introducing himself, Otto shows the requisition to the captain; and casting off, the captain sets sail for Indianola. Will has not been on a ship for seven months; Otto sees that he revels in the rhythm of rising, rolling, falling, and rising again. He and the captain talk at length, and Will receives a tour of the small ship. This is exactly what Otto wants to happen. He needs someone with knowledge of ship handling to ensure that the loading is efficient but also safe and secure.

The trip takes two and a half hours. The *Breaker* ties up at the lower wharf in Indianola. The entire party walks down the wharf to the stack of ties. Sound Florida Pine stacked eight feet high. Agreeing as to where the ties will be placed on board, the captain returns to the ship to count the number placed at each location. John stands by at the wharf to answer questions from anyone in town. Otto walks down the street to deliver the requisition to Henry Runge, an officer of the railroad company that owns the rails and ties.

Henry is in his store waiting on a customer. Otto uses the time to survey the merchandise. He is surprised to see that cornmeal is three cents per pound, but flour is seven cents per pound. No wonder that Mary made cornbread instead of biscuits. Rice is twenty cents per pound. The senior mess, with rice and beans last night, ate high on the hog.

Henry Runge, completing the business with his customer, walks over, saying, "Good morning, Otto, what can I do for you?" Without knowing what the response would be, Otto hands him the requisition. Reading it through, Henry purses his lips together before commenting. "That's going to pose some problems, but you folks at the fort provide protection for Indianola, and we should do all we can to assist you. What are you going to do with this material?"

Otto explains about the mule railway to move supplies and heavy ordnance. This seems to convince Henry. He comments, "Actually, the railroad is bankrupt. I'd appreciate it if you did not pass that on to anyone but Dan Shea. We won't hear anything from the railroad.

I will present this to the state of Texas, and they will probably just bury it." Otto has the fleeting impression that whatever happened, Henry Runge, the entrepreneur, would benefit from it in some way. Shaking hands with Henry to seal the arrangement, Otto turns and walks back to the wharf.

Stopping at the pile of ties, he says to John, "Why don't you visit your family briefly? I'll go with the shipment back to the fort and return to pick you up on the next trip, say about four o'clock." That is delightful news to John, who wastes no time in walking to Mary's house.

The loading continues, and Otto leads Will aside, asking if the stowage is safe for the return voyage. Will says, "We can load two more trips, and then I think we should sail."

Nodding, Otto walks over to the captain, asking, "How many ties do we have aboard?"

"About a hundred and twenty." Otto looks at the deck and sees three piles of the same size and a fourth short about ten ties.

"What would you think of sailing when we get that fourth stack full?" The captain does not want to overload his ship with deck cargo. He says, "That's fine. We will be reasonably trimmed." Otto thinks, *He's paid by the day—he has no need to rush.*

The trip back to the fort goes smoothly. Off-loading takes a little experimentation with who would stand where, but when that is settled, it goes quickly. The return trip is smooth. When they tie up at the wharf, John is not there, but he shows up halfway through the next loading, smiling and telegraphing his thanks to Otto, who asks, "Can you take on Will's work at the fort this time so that he could stay over? We can then pick him up here tomorrow morning."

John responds, "That's a great idea. Did you know that he and Frances Dickerson have announced their engagement?"

"No. All I know is that she was 'terribly smitten' by him."

Otto calls Will over and explains the plan. His huge smile shows he could hardly believe he is this lucky. Pulling a small note pad out of his pocket, Otto writes a twenty-four-hour pass, signs, and hands it to Will. John says, "Why don't you take off now? I'm not too old to do a little work, and Frances will be delighted to see you." He did. She was.

They return to the fort, and after unloading, the schooner sails around to the dock at Saluria.

Loading of ties is completed in the first trip of the next day. Loading of rails requires tools, specifically rail-lifting tongs that permit men to grab and lift a rail. After some searching, Otto finds the tongs in the warehouse at the foot of the wharf. There he also finds the tie plates, spikes, rail connectors, and bolts to complete the job. There is also a handcart used by workmen to travel short distances on the railroad. Otto thinks that would be ideal for the mule cart.

All of these materials are stacked at the fort two days later, and the tired crew is ready to start the survey. Signing the invoice for the captain, Otto thanks him for a satisfactory job of transport. The captain remarks that the five-hundred-foot line must be the shortest railroad in the west, and he is glad to be part of its construction.

The following day, the crew begins their survey to create two short-level sections of one-rail length at each end of the track and a five-hundred-foot run in between. This is marked off with stakes cut to the proper height every fifty feet on the embankment. The fifty men from Reuss's company begin to move and smooth the broken shell and sand from the beach to create the embankment. When the desired slope is achieved, the men, lacking a roller, march up and down it repeatedly to pack the material. This is accompanied with a comic and exaggerated set of commands, sometimes in English, sometimes in German. Finally, a mule is hitched to a pair of ties, which were pulled up and down the slope until it is smooth.

The men lay ties every three feet on the embankment. Two "rail gauges" are cut to ensure an accurate distance between the rails. Tie plates are laid on the ties, followed by the rails themselves with the rail gauges ensuring the proper spacing. The next step becomes a comic relief as the men try their skill at driving spikes into the ties with the long-handled hammers. Two men drive two spikes on a single plate. Because of the shape and angle of the head of the spike, it is necessary to drive the spike from the opposite side of the rail. This means the hammer head has to be long enough to reach over the rail, about eight inches. This long head makes accurate driving difficult. For some men, the skill comes naturally. For the rest, hitting the spike head solidly seems impossible. Shouts were heard: "Helmut, you are supposed to hit the iron thing, not the wooden one" and "I'd never ask you to cut off a chickens head, Klaus." After half an hour of jeers and laughter, the group receiving the kidding is assigned to coupling the rails together using connectors, nuts, and bolts. The other group settles down to drive spikes. The railroad progresses with surprising speed.

Late in the day, the last spike is driven, and a loud cheer rises from the crew. The shout of "Shortest railroad in Texas" brings immediate laughter wherever it is heard in the fort. Reuss comes to see the progress and marvels at the ability of youth to find humor in the simplest of achievements or the bleakest of prospects. He is careful not to voice that observation and instead says, "Otto, you've done it! A splendid job!"

* * *

That night in the senior officers' mess, with Garland attending, Bletchley remarks, "Today, my crew of slaves achieved an excavation of one and one-fourth yards of sand per man-hour. That's a significant improvement over the usual benchmark of one yard per man. I think that shows the power of slavery as a working arrangement. I'm thankful that we are fighting to preserve that arrangement."

Shea's face turns a deep crimson. Garland looks startled and glances back and forth from Shea to Bletchley. Reuss looks sternly at Bletchley, saying, "Mr. Bletchley, I believe you have been requested previously not to broach that subject in this mess. I am triply appalled. First, you have abused your slaves so severely that I've had to attend medically to two of them today. Second, you feel that this accomplishment is worth bragging about in front of a guest in our mess. Third, you have specifically entered a topic that Major Shea has prohibited in his mess. Sir, I leave my view of you to your own imagination."

This outburst is followed by a brief silence, but the expressions on the faces of the men indicate total agreement with Reuss. Vernon speaks. "Gentlemen, I offer an apology to our guest on behalf of all of us for this unseemly exchange. Let us put it behind us and enjoy our community and this excellent dinner."

Vernon steers the topic from the construction of the fort to organizational changes in the Confederate States Army. Headquarters for the Texas district had recently been moved from Galveston to Houston. Colonel Garland elicits chuckles from the fort's officers by describing the problems of desk-bound bureaucrats trying to work with actual material rather than just words. One politically appointed colonel wrote an order for a wagon to transport a 5,600-pound siege gun to a new location. The wagon would have collapsed at about one thousand pounds load. A sergeant in the artillery company suggested that maybe they should just lift the wagon onto the gun and transport it that way. When the colonel issued another idiotic order, a paper appeared in his inbound stack ordering that his desk be moved to the stables. In brisk efficiency, he signed it. In equally brisk fashion early next morning, the move is made. The colonel did not find his desk for three days. That story brings huge laughs.

The meeting breaks up with several men starting games of whist. Reuss and Otto walk together to their tent. For once, Reuss is quiet, and it is Otto who breaks the silence. "That was a well-merited speech you made. Do you suppose that Bletchley will ever see himself as the rest of us do?"

Reuss fills and lights his pipe before responding, "Bletchley is a one-track idiot. Only one idea is allowed in his mind at a time. I doubt that he is capable of looking into himself. Someday, that one track will carry him to his own destruction. I hope I'm not nearby when that happens."

* * *

The following day, Otto and his survey crew prepare to test the new railway. Maggie, the mule fitted with a wagon harness is led down to the beach end of the railway. In contrast to her usual willing manner, she refuses to step onto the tracks and be coupled to the handcart. This causes a discussion among the crew until John says, "She's afraid of the ties. It must look like a cattle guard to her." That seemed plausible, and as a test, sand is shoveled between the rails until the ties are hidden. This cures the problem, and Maggie is harnessed to the cart. With a tug on the lead, she starts up the tracks but stops again where the ties are visible. Otto chuckles, saying, "All right, Maggie, you win. We'll fill the entire line with sand." They did, and Maggie inaugurates the SRT, or shortest railroad in Texas. Colonel Garland is summoned, and Maggie performs for him. The colonel pats her neck and compliments Otto and his men for a job well done.

* * *

In January, the fortifications and trenches are finished. The entire three hundred men of the fort assemble in formation on the small quadrangle west of the bombproof dugout to hear the place commissioned as Fort Esperanza. In Spanish, the word means "hope." The junior officers feel it is appropriate in recognition of Indianola's promise as a major hub of commerce. Reuss, standing at attention in front of his company with his short artillerist's sword in front of his face, turns his eyes upward and silently prays that the hope is not a forlorn one.

Part II

Chapter Seven

January 25, 1862

John W. Kittredge captained a commercial steamship trading between Galveston and the Mexican border for several years before the war. Basically a gambler, he grew wealthy from a succession of clever trades. When he volunteered his services, the Union navy was pleased to make him volunteer lieutenant and captain of the bark *Arthur,* sending him out to catch Confederate blockade runners. The principle was "use one to catch one."

On December 11, 1861, at the New York Navy Yard, he stands at attention in a new uniform, his gray-tinged van Dyke beard combed by a fresh wind, which brings a fishy smell from the East River. His status as captain is confirmed to the assembled crew. The bugles blow, and the ship's company is dismissed to watch stations. This crew includes several extra master's mates, who would serve as captains aboard captured vessels that would be sent back to New York. There is also an extralarge crew to provide men to serve these vessels on their return trip.

In his cabin, Kittredge reflects that thus far, the detailed planning has paid off. He is ready to achieve his fortune once he establishes unquestioned control of this ship. A month later, the ship arrives off the Texas coast to open the most active period of blockading the Union mounted during the war.

* * *

Kittredge stands solidly on his quarterdeck. The new canvas sails are nicely bowed with a fresh southwest breeze. The teak deck is clean and clear of equipment except for the guns and launches.

The bow cleaves the green water of the Gulf approximately three miles offshore, and the odor of clean salt water is in the wind. All is as he wishes it to be aboard his ship. An excellent breakfast warms his stomach, and his nerves are in the relaxed but attentive state that he favors.

He addresses his first mate, "Mark that black lighthouse," gesturing a point off the port bow. "That is the light for Pass Cavallo. Our orders are to sail between there and Corpus Christi sixty-five miles to the southwest." Looking straight at the man, he asks, "Is that clear?"

The officer knows the drill, learned in the month since leaving New York. He stands erect and says clearly, "Yes, sir." On one hand, he, a career navy officer, resents this "civilian"; on the other, he must admit that Kittredge has repeatedly shown that he runs a very tight ship. His orders are a model of clarity.

Kittredge continues, "The pass at Cavallo has ten feet of water and that at Corpus has only five. As you well know, we draw fourteen feet and so must do our work outside the bar in the Gulf." His lips compress, and with head bowed slightly, he considers what he views as a stupid oversight in the formation of his squadron. Omission of shallow-draft vessels excludes him from pursuit of ships into the bays. That is now the major traffic route of the Confederacy, a long intracoastal waterway that extends from Pass Cavallo to the Mexican border. It will do no good and some harm to express these feelings to his crew.

With head raised, he smiles slightly and continues, "I hope to be joined shortly by shallow-draft ships, which can work inside the bays. For now, we will have to catch blockade runners before they attempt to cross the bar. There is a fort at Pass Cavallo and also at Corpus. I can see no profit in picking a fight with a fort until we have smaller ships with the ability to land infantry and capture it."

The executive officer knows what is going through the captain's mind and, putting a knowledgeable expression on his face, says, "I understand, sir."

Kittredge studies him for a moment and, smiling, says, "Yes, I believe you do. Please call me when you raise a sail." He turns and strides to his cabin. The officer considers briefly that his captain has distinctly said "when" not "if" you raise a sail.

* * *

The following morning, with the ship only twenty-four hours on station, the officer of the deck (OOD) leans against a shroud line to steady his telescope in response to the shout "Sail ho!" from the masthead lookout. A call is sent for Kittredge. They are seventeen miles north of Pass Cavallo and have just made their turn to go southward. There is a whirlwind of action as Kittredge orders general quarters and prepares two cutters for launching. The first mate will command one, and the second mate the other. Their job will be to board the Confederate ship and examine her cargo.

They do not want the ship run ashore and burned by the Confederates. That would permit the men to escape and deny the cargo to the Union. The cargo could be claimed as spoils and sold, with the proceeds going to the officers and crew of the *Arthur* only if it was the property of the Confederate States of America. Some crews even carried stencils with the letters "CSA" so that questionable goods could be marked and thus become spoils. Some infantry units in coastal areas claimed that CSA stood for "Cotton Stealing Association."

Kittredge orders the thirty-pounder rifled Parrott gun loaded with solid shot. His face a mask of concentration, he shouts, "Fire!" The round splashes in front of the vessel, which continues its run toward shore. He orders, "Helm to port. Come over between the ship and the shore." Then, "Load with shell, cut the fuse to explode in front of him." This produced an air burst high and plainly in sight. As the *Arthur* pulls closer, he orders, "Load with solid and put a round through his mainsail." The explosion is followed by a rip in the vessel's sail, which the wind causes to flap noisily. This cavalier style of shooting convinces the vessel's master to run up the Confederate flag and heave to. The first mate brings his launch alongside the vessel and, with drawn pistol, boards her. There is no saluting or courtesies. The pistol is pointed straight at the midsection of the man he takes to be captain as he says, "Damn you, sir. Why did you not heave to at the first shot? You have made us waste powder on your miserable vessel and poor person. Your ship and cargo are now the property of the United States Navy. How many crewmen do you have?"

"Two, sir, all that you see on deck."

"I thought I saw another man when we fired on you."

"That is one of two passengers."

"Do you have firearms aboard?"

"No, sir."

"Very well. Bring the passengers on deck and let me see the manifest."

Turning to the launch and pointing, he says, "You three come aboard and bring your arms." This is done just as two men and the captain appear in the companionway stepping onto the deck. The captain, handing over the manifest, stands stiffly, wondering if he would be shot for failure to stop at the first round. The first mate reads. He smiles to find a cargo of tobacco and coffee bound for Indianola out of Vera Cruz, Mexico. This is high-value cargo. His share will be significant. Kittredge has the right idea, even if he is a "civilian."

The vessel's captain, two crew, and passengers are asked if they wished to sign an oath of allegiance to the United States and go north with the ship. One of the crew volunteers. The others are ordered into the launch to be taken to the *Arthur*. The vessel becomes a prize, which the first mate and his crew of four will sail to New York.

Kittredge initially envisions a sizable credit to his bank account and smiles broadly while stroking his pointed beard as he reads the manifest of coffee and tobacco. That pleasure disappears as he reads further and finds that the manifest specifically names the owner of the cargo, and it is not the CSA. Manifests can become lost, but the named owner is one of the passengers aboard the ship and thus officially a prisoner. Kittredge might be greedy, but he is an honorable man. He did what regulations specify and sends both the manifest and the owner with the vessel to New York for adjudication of the spoils. Well, he thinks that's a lost profit, but there's no reason to spoil the whole game. There's more to be had on this coast.

In the following month, his frustration rises as he repeatedly sails up and down the islands, seeing coastal vessels that are beyond his reach in the bays at Corpus or Aransas. He tries sending the launches in by themselves, and this works after a fashion, but most ships simply sail away from the launches when his crews become exhausted by the extended rowing. Slowly, a small store of captured cargo builds up at the camp he establishes on St. Joseph Island. This is not the scale of spoils he envisioned but still it is profit.

* * *

The dispatch boat comes over the horizon flying the Union ensign and heading straight for the *Arthur.* When it comes alongside, the boat captain raises a speaking trumpet and hails, "Dispatches for Captain Kittredge." Both vessels heave to. An officer and two seamen put out from the dispatch boat. On board the *Arthur,* the officer of the deck orders a rope ladder over the side and sends a man to notify the captain.

When the dinghy comes alongside, its officer stands, shouting, "Permission to come aboard with dispatches for Captain Kittredge." Permission is granted. He climbs the Jacobs ladder to the deck, salutes first the ensign and then the OOD. Extracting a sealed envelope from a rubberized canvas bag, he hands it to the waiting Kittredge.

The envelope is quickly opened, and a broad smile spreads across the captain's face as he reads. He hands a stack of envelopes to the dispatch boat's officer, saying, "Send these to Key West." Then turning to the OOD, he orders, "Conference of the officers and mates in thirty minutes in my cabin."

* * *

Adm. David Glasgow Farragut has assigned him the yacht *Corpheus* purchased from the prize court in Key West, the screw gunboat *Sachem,* and a lugger *General Butler,* all armed and capable of operations in the shallow waters of the Texas bays. At last, reason has prevailed, and he has the necessary force to carry out his game. He sits a little straighter in his chair, and a warmth spreads through his torso as he thinks of the prospects with this force.

Farragut believes he has reason to favor Kittredge. His supply of career naval officers grew up in the service without fighting a war in fifty years. Their ingrained motivation is to stay out of trouble. Kittredge, with the venality of a merchant captain, goes out and finds trouble if it is profitable. That audacity is precisely what Farragut wants and finds lacking in his career officers.

Sitting at the table in his cabin, Kittredge watches as his officers and mates file in and stand in front of him. His face is a picture of satisfaction as he rises, saying, "Gentlemen, I have good news for all of us. This dispatch changes our orders. We will be joined by the *Corpheus* and two shallow-draft gunboats. Our orders are to pay particular attention to the coastal traffic in the area of Corpus Christi." Shifting to his chair, he places the order flat on his desk and, with a more serious mien, says, "Our method of operation will be to keep *Arthur* outside the bar and dispatch the shallow-draft ships and two launches into the bay. When a Confederate vessel is seen, the gunboats will fire on her, bringing her to a stop. Then the launches will approach and board, placing a prize crew and master on the vessel."

A quick glance confirmed that the prospect of spoils money is at the top of everyone's mind. Convinced that no more motivation is necessary, he continues, "The prisoners will be transferred to the *Arthur.* If the cargo is small, we will off-load it at the camp on St. Joseph Island. If the cargo is large, we will send both it and the vessel directly to New York as spoils. The smaller cargoes will be stored at the camp until there is enough to call in a deep-water ship from Key West."

His questioning glance locks on each of the men. He sees no questions. Nodding, he begins again, "We have much to do. I particularly want a good choice of men for the boats. Each launch must have at least two sharpshooters and an experienced prize crew. Each will be commanded by the man who will serve as the master of its prize vessel. Is all that clear?" It is completely clear and very promising.

* * *

Kittredge begins his plan by sending the gunboats and launches into Aransas Bay, adjoining the harbor of Corpus Christi. The plan works just as envisioned, and two small ships are captured. Their cargoes are off-loaded at St. Joseph Island. In the next month, the cargo store grows, and the men begin to have visions of snug homes overlooking the beaches of Maine or Massachusetts. At the price of $400 per bale for cotton, a cargo of one hundred bales will yield spoils money sufficient for a captain to buy a two-story home outright, and even the lowliest crewman could make a down payment.

Chapter Eight

February 10, 1862

News of Kittredge's success makes its way to Fort Esperanza, where Shea sits at his table in the bombproof area, watching gusts of rain blow past the entrance as a squall plays out in the Gulf. Sand blows around the corner of the fortification, building a pile, which tries to hide the support post. He sits deep in thought with his chin on his chest as Captain Bletchley enters, asking, "You sent for me?"

Shea gestures to a chair and, when Bletchley is seated, says, "John, I'd like to discuss a plan with you." Bletchley sits and looks as interested as he can manage. Shea's plans are never visible to him until they are explained in detail. Shea, putting on his best face, continues, "I want to send a small force down to St. Joseph Island to upset the activities of a Union blockader and recover the goods he's plundered from Confederate ships. Could you furnish me with twenty of your men and one officer to make the trip and provide support for the capture? We will be using mules and a chartered sloop to provide the transport."

Bletchley's face shows concentration and slowly turns red, a scowl covers it as he says with formality, "My orders are to defend this fort. I don't believe that extends to an offensive operation sixty miles down the coast."

Shea clamps his lips shut to contain the anger he feels surging through his body. After a moment, he says, "You report to the Eighth Texas Infantry to San Antonio?" Bletchley nodded in confirmation. Shea thinks to himself, *And I report to General Hebert in Galveston. What a hell of a way to run a war. Neither infantry nor artillery can be effective without the other, but each has orders through a separate command. Coordination is impossible. Nothing would be gained by taking this to a higher level.* He carefully avoided verbalizing that thought, saying instead, "Thank you, John." To his orderly sergeant, he says, "Please ask Reuss and Schnaubert to come in."

Waiting, Shea thinks on a peculiarity of the Germans in Texas. He has seen it repeatedly at New Braunfels, Fredericksburg, and even San Antonio. Wherever they gathered, they had a rifle range for shooting contests. Maybe that came from serving their dukes and princes in the German wars. Whatever its source, he thinks, *It's going to serve well if I must create my own infantry.*

Reuss and Otto arrive together and are offered chairs. They sit looking relaxed but attentive. Shea, turning to Reuss, says, "John, would your oath of service cover an operation to strike the Union blockaders at their sanctuary on St. Joseph Island sixty miles from this fort?"

Reuss looks puzzled then says, "Dan, our oath is to fight the enemy. We are under your command, and it's your call whether we strike them here or some other place. The fort is just where we're quartered."

Shea glances questioningly at Otto, who responds, "I agree 100 percent with Reuss." Shea relaxes; at least someone understands the fundamentals of tactics and strategy. Leaning forward, he outlines his plan. He wants eight sharpshooters and an officer mounted on mules to make the trip to St. Joseph Island supported by a sloop and an infantry platoon, which he will request from the local company in Corpus Christi. The marksmen will be used to panic the Yankees from a distance who will then flee into the arms of the infantry and be made prisoner. He hopes at the least to capture the looted cargo that the Union holds. With luck and the right timing, he might capture their leader Kittredge himself.

He sits a little straighter, saying, "If I remember correctly, your company has eighty-nine rifled muskets that were captured from the Yankees at Green Lake. I'd like you to take the best ten of those and the best eight sharpshooters from your company and prepare for an operation in about two weeks. Would it be possible for Otto to lead that detail?" Both Reuss and Otto agree.

* * *

In the next week, Reuss's company experiences a delightful relief from drill and inspection. The men who are thought to be the top-ten shooters fire the eight-nine muskets and select the ten best. Then those men who wanted to compete to be named marksman fire shots from each of the ten rifles at one hundred yards. There is cheering and jeering, and side bets are placed. Men from the other companies come to watch in envy at the great competition. Finally, the top-ten scorers are chosen, and each receives one of the rifles and the title of marksman. They then take on additional training at three hundred and four hundred yards over the next three days and are then pronounced ready.

Otto spends the period poring over the charts of St. Joseph Island and Cedar Bayou that lie between it and their own Mustang Island. Shea sends a message to the commander of the infantry company closest to St. Joseph Island, saying that he anticipates calling for support by a platoon in the near future for an action on St. Joseph Island. He will send a message by boat when the time comes.

* * *

On the appointed day, the small force, including Otto and Shea himself, mounting their mules, take the beach road south. The sloop follows their progress from the bay. At Cedar Bayou, the men swim the mules over at slack tide, and the sloop takes the rifles and powder across. Then waiting until dark, the men ride silently on the bay side of the island until they are opposite the Union camp. There they dismount and, creeping through the sandhills, approach the camp on the Gulf side. Through field glasses, Shea can count twenty-two men gathered around the campfire. He is sure from the uniforms that none of them is Kittredge. However, with infantry support, he will at least take the camp and prisoners. If the prisoners are visible to the ship offshore, she will likely not use her guns to shell the position. He sends a message back for the sloop to take across the bay to the captain commanding the infantry company. It requests support of one platoon to return on the sloop and, with his men, take the Yankee position. He settles down to wait.

Three hours later, a message is brought back by the sloop. Shea crawls well back from the forward position. Under a blanket, lighting a candle, he reads the message. When the meaning sinks in, his stomach wrenches tightly, and his fist beats slowly on the sand. The message reads:

> *I have the honor of receiving your note requesting support of a platoon from my company. I regret to inform you that is not possible, as it would weaken my force at the point that I am ordered to guard. It would also expose my platoon to shelling by the Union bark beyond the bar.*
>
> *Respectfully,*
> *Your obedient servant*

* * *

Shea, with Otto and the eight anguished marksmen, arrive back at the fort two days after their futile attempt to attack the camp on St. Joseph Island. Otto directs the care of the men and mules, while Shea goes directly to his tent, scribbling a note and calling for his orderly sergeant to deliver it to the mess. Tugging off his boots, he lies down on the cot and stares unblinking at the canvas roof.

Reuss is in the mess when the orderly sergeant hands him the paper. Unrolling it, he reads the brief message and, with a frown, says to the assembled officers, "Dan wants us to dine without him tonight. Please, let us go ahead." Otto's absence worries him too. He saw their arrival. The dark look on Shea's face had deflected him away from a welcoming greeting and the question "How did it go?" He has never seen such an expression of disgust and felt that it would be best to talk to Shea later.

With dinner over, Reuss goes to his hospital room and, taking a key, opens the medical stores box. His hand stops over a bottle of medical alcohol and then shifts to a bottle of Kentucky bourbon, which he selects, and then locks the box. Taking two glasses from the mess, he walks to Shea's tent. There is neither noise nor light inside. Lifting the flap, he sees Shea on the bed, still in uniform and staring upward without blinking. Lighting a candle, he bends to examine his patient. The veins on Shea's forehead are pulsing. He says in a soft voice, "Dan, your doctor is here making a house call with a prescription of medical alcohol to ward off a stroke. I don't have any Irish whiskey, but twelve-year-old bourbon should suffice." He pours three fingers of whiskey into each of the glasses and, setting them on the table, puts a hand behind Shea's back and, lifting him up, says, "I'm not going to pour it down your throat. The least you could do is sit up." Shea downs half of the glass, and his eyes began to blink. In another minute, he finishes the other half and exhales loudly, saying, "Damn him, damn him."

Reuss starts in on his own glass, waiting to see if there is more coming. He prompts, "You mean Kittredge?"

Shea looks at him as if the question is stupid. In a moment, he exhales and says, quietly, "No, I mean the damn infantry captain—maybe I mean myself."

Reuss observes that the veins are pulsing less violently, and the head is now turning to observe the inside of the tent. Thinking that his patient is ready to unload, he says simply, "What happened, Dan?"

Indicating that a second dose is required, Shea holds out the glass. When it is filled, he recounts the failed mission. His disgust with both himself and the divided command that foiled his effort is evident. When the second glass is empty, Reuss can see no profit in continuing the inquiry into the mission and, shifting track, asks, "What do you hope to do after the war is over, Dan? I dream of seeing my boy through med school and maybe the two of us having a joint practice. What's your dream?"

At first, Shea recoils at the sudden shift in topic, but the six fingers of bourbon allow a graceful slide, and he begins, "If the Confederacy wins this war, I'll have established enough rank to stay in the army and live out my days in a position of command. If the Confederacy loses, God forbid, I still have something going for me." Lying back against the pillow, he continues, "Indianola will become a prominent shipping hub. With my experience as a steamboat captain and a military commander, I should be able to raise a shipping company that would provide a sizable profit. The Union will need Indianola to supply the West and eventually California. Voyages around Cape Horn will become a thing of the past when you can ship to the port here and then by rail to California."

After a pause, Shea resumes, "I knew of Kittredge before the war, John. He is clever and aggressive. He had a reputation for a fast ship. That speed was achieved at times with the safety valve tied down. Anyway, he is an ambitious and hard-driving captain—I wish that he was on our side." Reuss marvels at the similarity of Shea and Kittredge and the events that brought them to be opponents in this conflict.

Shea's last comment is said with some slowness, then with a great sigh, he lies back on the cot and closes his eyes. Reuss finds a blanket and covers him up to the chin. Returning the bourbon to the medical locker, he walks slowly to his own tent and finds Otto rolled in blankets and sound asleep. Well, he thinks there is the difference between command and first officer. The commander needs a little help from his friends to find sleep. The first officer is simply exhausted.

* * *

On February 28, insult is added to Shea's injury when the bark *Arthur* appears off Matagorda Island on the Gulf side of Fort Esperanza. A boat is lowered and rowed ashore under a flag of truce. Shea and Reuss ride down to the shore and are astounded to see Kittredge step onto the island. His first question is "Who is in charge here?"

Shea responds, "I am in charge of this fort."

"Sir, I am the captain of that bark, and if I wished, I could destroy your fort. However, my orders require that I not shell you unless I am fired upon."

Shea's stomach clenches at this bombast. Evidently, the man does not recognize him as a fellow prewar captain. He will not give the satisfaction of recognition either. Taking a deep breath, he asks simply, "Why are you here?"

Kittredge replies that he wishes to release on parole the captain of a schooner he captured, also his invalid wife. Shea replies, "That is agreeable. I will have her carried to Saluria, where her husband can care for her."

Kittredge says with pride and an erect carriage, "I know the number and exact caliber of your guns, Captain Shea. I get the latest Texas papers, and my government takes care that I'm kept informed of your movements."

Shea is shocked but, on reflection, not surprised. There are groups in Texas that distinctly favored the Union. This furthers his anguish, but his countenance remains fixed. He says slowly and distinctly, "The white flag will be honored as long as it flies, but if it is taken in, there will be shots." Nodding agreement, Kittredge turns and, stepping into his boat, returns to the bark.

Reuss reflects on these two men whose motivations are similar despite the bombastic style of one and the gentlemanly manner of the other.

* * *

They return to the fort where Otto has crews standing by the guns with the caissons of ammunition immediately to the rear. Shea calls Otto over, saying with compressed lips, "Please observe that bark. If the white flag drops, commence firing solid shot at its hull and do not stop until it is sunk or out of range." Turning, he storms away to his tent.

The bark sails out of range and then drops the white flag, turning to head for Corpus Christi. In his report of the event, Shea later writes: "*The captain's wife was indeed an invalid as was shown by the weakness of her nether regions. However, this weakness did not extend to her tongue, which she used with strong effect on her husband.*"

* * *

The word comes to Shea in March that the orders to the infantry at Aransas Pass have changed to emphasize capturing J. W. Kittredge rather than standing on shore and waiting to be attacked. A new company commander, Capt. John Ireland, is specifically charged with the task. Shea is elated and selects two of the marksmen, with Reuss, to make a trip to Aransas and confer with Ireland.

After a brief introduction, Shea and Reuss are taken to the company command post in a large home on a cliff overlooking Aransas Bay. The house was evacuated by the owner when Union ships showed up in the bay. The Confederacy occupies it, making it headquarters for an infantry battalion. The exterior has an extensive flower garden, now deserted but volunteering blossoms to its absent owners. The interior is now definitely military, clean, and orderly. A light breeze rustles the curtains on an open window in the bedroom that serves as the company office. Seating himself, Shea says, "Captain Ireland, I heartily endorse your effort to capture Kittredge. He's been a thorn in our side for too long. I have brought two of my marksmen to illustrate what we can do at a distance of four hundred yards. I offer you the entire team of eight for your project."

Ireland beams, saying, "Word of your marksman project preceded you. I thought it an excellent idea, so we held a similar competition among the men of my company. It received great enthusiasm, and we have a team of ten crack shots that are ready to take on Kittredge. I really have to compliment you on that idea. The effect of precision shooting at four hundred to five hundred yards will panic the enemy."

Shea feels mixed emotions. He revels at the targeting of Kittredge by an effective force but sees his chance to personally contribute slipping away. Hoping to recover some role, he asks, "Will you let us give a demonstration of our marksmanship?"

"Of course, my men would like to see that."

*   *   *

Targets are set up at four hundred yards, and Shea's two men slowly squeeze off ten shots, with all ten piercing the man-sized center of the target. Reuss, beaming, says, "That should strike fear in the heart of any Union troops that were left standing."

Ireland readily agreed, motioning to two of his men. They take up the positions vacated by Shea's marksmen. Quiet prevails as breathing stops. Then a shot rings out. A hit on the target is announced by the soldier with a telescope. Nine shots followed all hits.

Ireland smiles confidently at Shea, saying, "You see, we have deer hunters in Seguin and New Braunfels just as you have in Indianola. Your offer is a gracious one, but as you can imagine, my men will never forgive me if I turned that plum assignment over to your men. However, if you want to come along as an observer, I'd be honored and privileged to have you personally on the excursion."

Shea considers that and imagines himself as "observer" in the capture of Kittredge. Thinking that he would be commander or nothing, he smiles at Ireland, saying, "You are to be complimented. I look forward to hearing of your accomplishments and will not add to your chores by tagging along as observer."

Reuss thinks, *Ireland is very smooth. I hope I see more of this fellow. I expect that Shea is thinking that someday, Ireland will report to him, and together they will do great things.*

* * *

At noon on April 21, the *Arthur* launches three cutters, with Kittredge in personal charge. In Aransas Bay, the cutters fire on and stop a schooner. The men in one cutter board her to examine the cargo. Then two sloops are sighted. The Union crew simply "unbends" the schooner's sails and, putting them in one of the cutters, takes out after the two sloops, leaving the schooner helpless with its crew aboard. No sooner are the two sloops captured than a third appears. The telescope proves this one to be different, as it contains a large group of riflemen. The two captured sloops are sworn to proceed to a Union dock. Naturally, they sail the other way as soon as they are out of range.

Fearing capture by the Confederate sloop, the Union boats pull for St. Joseph Island. There they run the boats ashore and take up position on the bay side of the island. A schooner joins the Confederate sloop, then a second sloop, all carrying Confederate infantry. They land on the beach about one thousand yards from the Union force. The Union troops fire with no effect, but the Confederate fire from Ireland's marksmen kills one of their number at that great distance. This unnerves the Union force, which flees across the island to summon the *Arthur* for protection and transport. Boats are put out from the bark to rescue the soldiers and prevent them from abandoning the accumulated spoils.

The Confederate force captures the three Union cutters and all of their equipment. Finding a full set of sails on board one of them, they correctly guess that a sail-less Confederate vessel is somewhere in the bay. They find it and, returning the sails, receive great thanks from the captain.

Ireland, pleased to capture the launches from the Union, still wants Kittredge.

Chapter Nine

July 1862

The brilliant sun rises in a virtually cloudless sky, promising the day would be a hot one. The afternoon breeze off of Corpus Christi Bay will alleviate that, but the guard at infantry battalion headquarters already has to wipe the sweat from his forehead at 9:00 a.m. He retreats to the dappled shade of an oak tree and patiently awaits his replacement.

The aroma of flowers from volunteer plants in the abandoned garden comes through the window into the room where John Ireland sits at a table, looking steadily at his first lieutenant. Ireland was a lawyer before forming his infantry company in Seguin, his lawyerly approach evidenced by the legal pad in front of him on the table. Addressing his companion, he muses, "Why did we fail to get Kittredge? He was not there. Neglect that. If he had been, I doubt we could have captured him."

The question prompts a reply. "We could not possibly attack that bunch once they went into the sandhills of the island. They spread out and were ready to pick us off one by one as soon as we moved."

Ireland rises to look out the window, enjoying the view of the bay. Thinking his way through the problem, he says, "Maybe we are wrong to try to go to them. How could we get a small group, including Kittredge, to come to us?—say, in a prepared position on the island. That way, we could be the group dispersed in the sandhills, and his group would be together with us surrounding them. What does he like that we could use to attract and trap him?"

"Loot, Confederate property to destroy?" asks the lieutenant. "Suppose we transport some cotton bales out where he can see them."

"That would be a little obvious," replies Ireland. "He would ask himself why the bales are in plain sight and who put them there. That would put him on guard, and we would be the ones on the defensive." In the silence, the window curtains stirred. The lieutenant spoke hesitantly, "There are still a few houses on St. Joseph Island that have not been burned or wrecked by the Yankees. Suppose we emplace ourselves around one of them in the sandhills. Let him see two of us go into the house. He would think that if we went in, there must be something worthwhile there. When he comes to take us prisoner and loot the place, our men can stand up and force his surrender."

"If he surrenders," replied Ireland, "we take him to the beach and get him off the island real quick. If he does not, we shoot him right there and all the men in his party. What's wrong with that plan?"

The better part of the afternoon is spent trying to find a fault in the plan. The only ones are minor. But, they conclude, it could only work once. They must be sure of Kittredge's presence on the island before trying it.

* * *

On several occasions, it seems that events are right for the plan; but in each event, something is missing, usually Kittredge. Then an unusual thing happens: Kittredge comes to Ireland.

On September 13, Captain Kittredge, under a flag of truce, sails into Corpus Christi Bay on the *Corpheus*. He enters on a southwest wind, the bow of the boat rising and falling on a following wave. Spray comes over the windward bow with a swishing sound. The sails, set close hauled, thrum steadily. Kittredge stands on the quarterdeck, watching for a truce boat to put out to meet him. Overhead, a large white flag flaps noisily.

When a small boat is seen leaving the dock with a similar white flag, Kittredge orders, "Continue for a half mile then come about into the wind and drop anchor." When this is accomplished, the

Corpheus is aligned with its starboard battery facing the small fort at Corpus. When the truce boat pulls alongside, Kittredge speaks with its master and boards for a trip to the fort.

Presenting himself to the fort's commander, he states, "My reason for the truce is to convey Judge Davis's family, Union sympathizers, from Corpus to New Orleans."

The commander, suspecting a ruse, says, "Captain, I will need ten days to get an answer from my superior in San Antonio."

Kittredge simply views this as ten days to spread havoc within the bay. Saluting the commander, he says, "I'll return for your answer, sir." He then sails fifteen miles down the bay to the saltworks at Laguna Madre.

* * *

Captain Ireland and a detachment of artillery are ashore watching Kittredge. When the *Corpheus* dropped anchor for the night, the infantry takes up position behind an abandoned house near the shore opposite the anchorage. Ireland tells his first lieutenant, "Have the men dig holes where they will be out of sight, then stay there all night."

The following morning, the ship shells the shore. The confederates, in their holes, experience no casualties. Convinced that the house is abandoned, Kittredge heads ashore in a launch with seven men in search of plunder. Ireland, sitting behind an oak tree, raises his telescope, careful to keep the lens in an area of shade to avoid sending any flashes to the enemy. He studies the launch carefully and says quietly to his lieutenant, "There are eight men aboard, and one is wearing a captain's uniform. I think we've got him. He is coming to us!"

The launch lands below the house, and the entire party climbs up the bank. When the Yankees arrive at the front yard of the house, Ireland's entire force of fifty men rise and challenge them. The Yankees, surprised and hopelessly outnumbered, drop their arms and surrender without a shot. The *Corpheus* opens fire on the entire party, Confederate and Yankee, but achieves no casualties. The Confederate artillery fires on the *Corpheus* with considerable advantage, owing to their location well above sea level. The ship decides to abandon the launch and sail out of range of the artillery. The launch is captured with all its equipment.

Ireland hustles his men and prisoners back from the shore and out of sight behind the cliffs, saying formally, "Captain Kittredge, allow me the honor and privilege to welcome you to the state of Texas."

Kittredge, not to be outdone, replies, "Today, I am your obedient servant, sir." He did not smile.

* * *

In a curious concession, probably a salute to Kittredge's audacity, a boat sent to the *Arthur* under a white flag picks up his clothing and personal effects. He signs a parole and goes to San Antonio for transportation to his exchange point. The men are sent directly for exchange. Kittredge, an honorable man, does not take another navy assignment. His capture takes the heart out of the blockading flotilla. Although they continue operations with moderate success, they never again achieve the audacity shown by their "civilian" Captain Kittredge.

The news of the capture spread rapidly through Texas. Nowhere did it generate greater pleasure than at Fort Esperanza. Shea, beside himself with joy, planned that sometime in the future, Ireland would serve under him.

PART III

CHAPTER TEN

October 15, 1862

The newspaper brings the story of the new head of the Trans-Mississippi District the preceding week. In the mess that evening, Vernon, now in command of the fort as a result of Shea's promotion, turns to Otto, saying, "I know very little of this new general Magruder, but I believe he commanded your old outfit, the First U.S. Artillery, what can you tell us about him?"

"He left to command West Point before I joined them, but his reputation lasted a long time. The men called him 'Prince John.'" This prompted a round of chuckles. Otto continues, "Some said the nickname came from his fancy uniforms. He always had a colorful item in addition to the regulation dress. Others said it reflected his love of the theater and dressing up in costumes. He staged a lot of plays and costume balls."

Reuss, laughing, says, "That may explain something. I understand during the peninsula campaign, when he defended Richmond under Lee, he marched his men around in a huge circle, in and out of a forest. There were a lot of different bugle calls and McClellan, the Union general, seeing regiment after regiment passing first one way and then another, concluded that Magruder had twice as many men as he actually commanded." Laughter bounced off the walls. When it quieted, Reuss continued, "I don't know what he did wrong or who he offended, but he's our man now. At least he's an outstanding artillerist."

* * *

The following morning, a rider arrives with Magruder's first orders. Vernon calls a conference of his officers in the bombproof shelter. Completing the ritual questions of health and stores, he says, "You all know that we have a new leader, Gen. John Bankhead Magruder. I have orders this morning, and we are left no doubt as to his intentions. The general feels that the Yankees are about to invade Texas, and he has ordered a 'scorched earth' policy to delay them in that conquest. Specifically, Major Shea is ordered to burn the railroad ties at Indianola to prevent their use in constructing a spur from the docks to the interior of the state. Shea wants us to carry out this action. I would like to discuss with you how we will go about this."

Captain Bletchley, his face a deep red, screams, "You can't do this! Those ties are the property of the Indianola Railroad Company."

Vernon glowers. "Mr. Bletchley, I have been given a direct order in writing. You will please refrain from telling me what I cannot do."

Bletchley, his face bordering on purple, steams ahead. "I am an investor in that company. I bought bonds with the proceeds from my plantation. Those ties are my property. I will protect them with all my personal ability."

Vernon, his own face reddening, says, "Let me have your pistol." Bletchley, puzzled, drew his pistol and passes it to Vernon, who continues, "Lieutenant Schnaubert, take this pistol and put Mr. Bletchley under arrest. Bletchley, it is very fortunate that you did not say you would use your troops to stop me from carrying out my orders. That would be rank insubordination, possibly treason, and unquestionably require a court martial. I will consider the charges later and advise you within forty-eight hours." A stunned silence filled the room.

Otto tries hard not to smile and thinks of the serious consequences if he were to shoot Bletchley. Standing, he escorts the captain to the guardhouse, ironically sheathed with stout ties requisitioned from the railroad stock at Indianola. Searching, he finds and removes a knife from Bletchley's pocket and unfastens his holster. Fortunately, Sgt. Samuel Clark stands duty as guard. He is very senior, reliable, and not burdened with a sense of humor. Otto turns over his prisoner, saying, "Sam, this man is to be kept prisoner until you have written orders from Captain Vernon to release him." Clark confirms the orders, and Otto hurries back to the conference.

Walking back to the dugout, he admires the pistol, a .44-caliber Colt Dragoon, manufactured at the pistol factory in Lavaca. Bletchley purchased it with his own funds when he organized the company. The pistol appears in good condition—why not? Bletchley has two slaves to serve and care for him. The belt and holster are good Texas leather. Slipping the belt on, he holsters the pistol just as he enters the bomb shelter.

* * *

Vernon describes the plans for burning the ties. "One of Bletchley's lieutenants will take his company to Indianola along with a detachment made up from the two artillery companies. They will collect, stack, and burn the ties. Shea, in command at Indianola, will lead the burning party." Vernon will be in charge of the fort, and Otto in charge of the artillery at the fort. "Reuss will take a single twelve-pounder and its crew and twenty men from his company to threaten any mob that might develop in the town. Shea has no intention of using it, but it will look persuasive." Vernon selected Reuss, sure that he would not use artillery against the civilians of his own town under any circumstances. It could be used to quell any mutiny that developed from Bletchley's men.

Otto could see that he and Vernon would be in charge of Bletchley and that Shea would be in a position to control Bletchley's troops if there were any problems. He did not anticipate that. The troops showed no great loyalty. Again, he marveled at Vernon's quickness in sorting out an action that he could not possibly have anticipated. His attention turned to his own duty at the fort.

* * *

Shea meets at the edge of town with a delegation of merchants who heard rumors and were concerned that the "scorched earth" policy might include burning the wharves and business district. In fact, the orders did thoughtlessly cover the wharves and some of the warehouses. Facing the merchants, Shea says, "I am prepared to argue that the wharves and warehouses are necessary to support the fort and thus request a change in my orders. Tonight's work will only be destruction of the 575,000 board feet of ties."

Henry Runge, merchant and investor in the railroad company, looks displeased but feels the trade of his warehouses against the railroad ties might be the best that he could get. He knows better than most that the railroad is already bankrupt. He tried to get funding from Germany and failed. With the civil war in full bloom, the railroad became a closed issue in his mind.

Reuss points the twelve-pounder up Water Street, and only the gun crew knows that there is nothing in front of the powder charge. It proves unnecessary. Little disturbance come from the town. Few persons had a direct investment in the railroad company, and everyone felt that the war had postponed the completion of the railroad connection into the unforeseeable future.

Shea makes one shrewd concession, saying to the citizens, "You are free to take ties for firewood, provided the wood is split and chopped short." This prompts a rush to get saws and axes and return for this gift of good Florida pine to use during the coming winter. The citizens' concern about destruction instantly changes to desire for advantage on the firewood giveaway.

Bletchley's men pile railroad ties into cribs eight feet high along the graded embankment that would have been the railroad. There are over thirty cribs, stretching for three hundred feet. Turpentine is spread on a few of the cribs at the windward end, and a pile of kindling is laid. Just before dark, Shea gives the order, and the fire blooms across the cribs. Citizens and soldiers alike watch in awe as the flames catch and then spread rapidly from one crib to the next.

The piles are sufficiently removed from the business buildings to prevent the fire jumping out of control, but the sight and roaring sound are frightening to the observers. The smoke carries a pungent odor of burning pitch.

Shea watches in anguish. He hoped the railroad connection to the growing port of Indianola would offer him a chance to raise a shipping company. Now that dream is literally going up in smoke. Still, he has a responsible position in the Confederate establishment with a chance of promotion. He carries out his orders even if they are against his dream.

* * *

At the fort, all eyes watch as darkness falls and the glow of the fire becomes visible on the horizon where Indianola stands. Otto watches, knowing that his chances as surveyor for the new railroad are disappearing into the smoke now rising over the orange glow.

Bletchley peeks through a gap in the ties that formed the heavy door of his prison. As the glow appears, he groans; and when the smoke rises, he bellows, "Wrong, wrong, wrong!"

Otto walks to the guardhouse to check on his prisoner. The pistol lies heavy in the holster at his right side. Sounds from inside the guardhouse are audible fifty yards away. Despite his hatred of Bletchley, he feels some sympathy. The man has just lost most of his fortune. Then his inner self tells him that fortune was made from slavery, and it should be the slaves crying. Not sure what, if anything to do, he simply nods to Sergeant Clark and asks, "Is everything well?"

"I would say so, sir."

CHAPTER ELEVEN

October 25, 1862

Otto stands in the town of La Salle, on the mainland opposite Saluria. His task is to examine the mules that were moved ashore to conserve both water and forage on the island. He finds them in good health and their harnesses in fine condition. Mounting his mule to return to the fort, he clamps his knees to its body. The government saddles never feel right. They have a narrow pommel and seem like a thin seat of leather on the mules back. In contrast, the typical Texas saddle is wider and has a pommel that he can fit his thighs to and a comfortable backrest. In a world that had plenty of hides and leather, the government saddles seem a poor economy. But they came as free property when the Union troops left Texas a year ago, and that saved money for the Confederacy.

Walking the mule in the direction of the ferry dock, he sees a horseman galloping in the same direction. Otto hails him, but the man will not stop and hurries past on his way. When he reaches the dock, the ferry is out in the bayou, taking the horseman to the fort and requiring Otto to wait for its return. Signaling to the ferryman, he dismounts to wait. An hour later, he is crossing the bayou; and the mule, recognizing the path home, is eager to go.

When he lands, another mounted man waiting for the ferry says, "Mr. Schnaubert, Major Vernon has sent me to find you. He wants to see you immediately."

"What's wrong?"

"I don't know, sir, but we've been ordered to get the mules into teams. The fort is like a beehive."

The description is apt. Men oil harnesses, and others load supply wagons and secure their covers. He can see men from his own company opening the caissons and loading ammunition. His guide offers to take care of the mule, and, dismounting, Otto walks quickly to headquarters.

* * *

Inside the bomb shelter, men come and go in rapid sequence. He steps to Vernon's field desk and waits to be acknowledged. Finally, looking up, he says, "Otto, take a look at this," pointing to a map of the Texas coast. "I have just received orders from Indianola. A large Union navy force is on its way down the coast. It should arrive here tomorrow. Our scouts tell us they have heavy ships, and some are loaded with infantry. My guess is that they are headed for us. The vessels draw too much water for the harbor at Corpus. I expect they will bombard us and try to interdict the coastal shipping in the bay. If I wanted to stop that traffic, Fort Esperanza is where I would head. If they get past us, they will have a good base for invading Texas, just as Magruder expected."

Now Otto understands the cause of the activity outside, and his anxiety rises. He hopes the guide hasn't unsaddled his mule, as he will likely need it the rest of the day and sometime into the future.

Vernon, sitting at his table in the dugout, stretches his cramped back and says, "We are ordered to bring two twelve-pounders to Indianola. They'll be joined there by a cavalry company from Victoria. I want you to take charge of that battery. Get under way as soon as you are loaded."

"Will we have infantry protection?"

"Yes, you and Reuss will lead the march from here with a detachment of Bletchley's infantry. Most of his company will stay here to protect the larger guns. I will be in charge of the fort, with Beyer in charge of the artillery. Shea is in charge at Indianola, and you will take your orders from him."

Otto marvels at the rapidity with which this change in command is implemented. It makes sense when Vernon says it, but clearly he must have thought this through on one of his frequent questions, *What do we do in the event that—?"*

"Otto, you should draw rations for two weeks and take about twenty men from your company in addition to the two gun crews. Load all the twelve-pounder ammunition that we have and take half of the powder. I think it would be wise to have an extra two wagons in case there are wounded. Take Lt. George French with you. Any questions?"

"Yes, sir, I take it we are going by road and not by boat from Saluria?"

Vernon confirms this, adding that he wants a junction with the cavalry outside Indianola if possible in the event the Yankees land troops before the artillery arrives. Lowering his head and in a confidential tone, he says, "Otto, don't be surprised if Shea sends you on to Lavaca. He and I have discussed this several times, and he doesn't think Indianola is defensible. I don't feel that strongly about it, but he has a point. There is nothing but flat land between Indianola and Lavaca. If your artillery gets caught on that road, there's no place to form a defense line." Vernon pauses, let out a long sigh, and continues, "The twelve-pounders won't be any good here or at Indianola against the Union ships, but they could be effective at Lavaca where the channel is narrow and shallow and land restricts maneuvering. That's just my view, take your orders from Shea."

* * *

Vernon dismisses him, and Otto feels the load of a dozen tasks fall on him and his company. Walking to the open ground of the fort, he surveys the action under way. Seeing John Noll, he motions to the sergeant and reviews the instructions received from Vernon. Noll has anticipated most of this, but they need to discuss the extra men beyond the gun crews. Otto says, "John, I want Will Moore to be with us. We will be firing at ships in harbor, and he can be a real help in anticipating their movement."

"Should we take any spares or extras?"

"We'll probably need parts for the wagons, if you can find space, throw in extra wheels and trees. We should also have one spare team of mules and the men that care for them. Fill in the additional men as you see fit. We have to be under way before dark, so send units over on the ferry as soon as each is ready. I'll be at the ferry landing on the shore side. We will form up there." Noll acknowledges this and moves to fulfill his tasks.

Otto finds George French and tells him of the plan and his assignment, "George, I want you to stay here at the fort and move things along as fast as possible. John Noll is selecting the men for the detachment. I'll be over in La Salle trying to find a map of the roads from there to Lavaca. I only know the road by the bay. If there's another road less exposed to bombardment from the bay, I'd like to know it. La Salle has a post office and delivers in that area. They may have a detail map. When the last unit is on the ferry, you bring up the rear." He goes to his tent to pack a saddlebag with necessities, an extra warm shirt, and two blankets.

As he closes the bag, he thinks about Vernon's words. It sounds like the fort stands a good chance of being abandoned. On further thought, he gathers up the surveying equipment and carries it to a nearby wagon, where it is loaded with the supply of rations. It would be a shame to lose his equipment to the Yankees. Memorizing the name of the driver, he smiles ironically, saying, "Be real careful and don't lose our supper."

He finds his guide who still has the mule and, thanking him, heads for the ferry. The mule is unhappy with being turned away so close to home but reluctantly boards the boat.

* * *

The post office does have a map, but volunteer help came from an old rider who delivered mail for ten years over western Calhoun County. He is full of tales of the way things were in the good old days but does furnish information on roads and bridges in between the history lessons. Otto makes notes directly on the map, but senses there are no real roads for artillery except the bay road. The rest are just cow trails interrupted by shallow bayous and questionable bridges. He had better make it through as quickly as possible and move back from the bay when he gets to Indianola. Getting caught in the open by the guns of the Union ships is a terrible prospect.

* * *

At the ferry landing, Otto sits astride his mule, watching teams pull the guns off the ferry and up the bank to the road. He twists in the saddle to gauge the height of the sun. The leather groans, and the mule snorts as he extends a hand at arm's length and counts six finger widths from the sun to the horizon—an hour and a half then fifteen minutes of twilight. He must be well under way before dark. Turning, he finds the junior lieutenant in charge of Bletchley's men, saying, "I want you to form up on the road and move out northward. If you find the unit behind you by more than two hundred yards, stop and wait for them to catch up."

The first gun and its caisson follow next, then the spare mules and the supply wagons. The second gun is late coming off the ferry, and the whole movement stops at the prescribed two hundred yards spacing. A sudden anger filled Otto's head, and he shouts at the young lieutenant, "For God's sake, get that gun up the hill and into line. We will be in a terrible fix if the Union ships find us all strung out like this with no place to form a defense."

The tardy gun and its caisson hustle into line, and the parade of squeaking wheels and snorting mules slowly moves forward. Reuss arrives on the last ferry and takes the lead, with Otto in front of Bletchley's men. Lieutenant French brings up the rear. At sundown, they are a little over four miles from the wharf in the middle of the treeless flats of southern Calhoun County, barely five feet above sea level. Otto's anxiety rises; clearly this is no place to camp. He says to Reuss, "We can't stop here. We are completely vulnerable to any ship in the bay. I think we'd do best to continue onto Indianola."

Reuss replies, "I agree completely. Would you just ride back along the line and see if we have any problems developing?"

"I'll do that," Otto replies.

The march continues through the night under a rising moon. They reach a spot one mile outside Indianola shortly before sunrise. A halt is called, and fires are started with driftwood brought up from the beach.

The weather is not freezing, but a fire is welcome after a night on the road. Otto unsaddles his mule and stakes it out in the saw grass. He joins Reuss at the small fire where a mush of cornmeal is beginning to puff steam. The heat of the fire feels good, and the odor of the steam reminds him of the missed dinner last night. Reuss motions him to sit and says, "I think we did reasonably well for a detachment that's not experienced in movement. We made about sixteen miles. French tells me there were no stragglers and surprisingly no breakdowns in the wagons. I have to hand it to our Germans—they take good care of their stock and machines. What do you make of our route for tomorrow, or is that today?"

"Well, I make it about twelve miles to Lavaca if we have to go there. I think we would do well to send a man ahead to contact the cavalry coming from Victoria and coordinate our movements."

Reuss considers this while removing and polishing his glasses, saying, "All right, send French on ahead. He should report to Captain Breckenridge, who is leading the cavalry. Shea will be in charge of the entire detachment when we join up. Who should we put in the rear-end position if we have to move without French?"

"I'd suggest Sgt. Sam Clark—he's very senior and well respected by the men. He's been married for eleven years and has raised some kids. He'll know how to handle any stragglers. He's also a farmer, so a broken wagon won't be a mystery to him."

"Good, now how would some of this mush do for breakfast?" Otto thinks that will do fine even if that is the fiftieth straight day he has cornmeal mush for breakfast.

* * *

French returns at midmorning, reporting that he had found Captain Breckenridge, who agreed to meet at their location. The junction will be shortly before noon. The detachment settles down to wait for developments at Fort Esperanza. It is not a long wait.

The dull boom of guns began about ten o'clock. The first sounds are the slow regular firing of the fort's twenty-four-pounders. Soon, this is joined by a random sequence of sounds from the Union ships. Otto counts and thinks, *My god, there must be fifteen or more shipboard guns, and I can hear air bursts over the fort.* This isn't encouraging. If the fort is outgunned 3 to 1, it will not hold out much beyond a day.

The sounds continue through the morning. Reuss paces back and forth and finally asks Otto to go into town and contact Shea to confirm that the twelve-pounders and the cavalry have joined up and ask for his orders. Otto saddles his mule and, with a slight modification of his instructions, loads it with the surveying equipment. Mary's house is on a direct route from their location to the downtown area where Shea is likely to be. A detour will add no more than ten minutes.

* * *

Otto knocks on the back door. When Mary appears, he gives her a huge hug and a warning that he has only a minute. Then unloading the surveying equipment, he hides it in the loft of the barn under a pile of hay. Giving Mary a second hug, he tells her that they are possibly going to be moved to Lavaca, and she should tell no one. He cautions her to stay out of downtown, as the Union may shell it later. Then a brief kiss and back onto the mule. Mary watches in amazement at the sudden turn of events. Hurrying indoors, she grabs Lina Katlyn up in her arms. Her breath comes in gasps. *What is the world coming to?* Her town attacked with cannon. *Don't tell anyone?* Her first reaction is anger—squint eyed, jaw clamped anger. Then after ten deep breaths, as her father had taught her, recalling that Otto said to stay home, she closes all the windows, draws the shades, changes Lina's diapers, and fixes a cup of corn coffee for herself.

* * *

Shea is indeed in his office downtown. He looks tired but smiles warmly, saying, "Otto, it's good to see you again. I wish the circumstances were better." When the information is passed about the junction with the cavalry, Shea pauses thoughtfully, running his hand through his thinning hair, then gives Otto a sealed envelope, instructing, "Please give this to Reuss and don't delay." Otto thinks it was good that he had stopped at the house on the way in. That way, he won't have to overtly disobey orders on the way back.

* * *

Returning to the encampment, Otto finds the captain and hands over the envelope. Reuss looks at him, asking, "Do you know what's in it?" A shake of the head confirmed that he doesn't. Slitting the envelope, Reuss extracts two sheets of paper and reads rapidly. He looks downcast and weary. With a deep sigh, he says, "We are ordered to move to a position in the business district of Indianola and, after a brief exchange of fire, go to a point of our choice to defend Lavaca. The fort will be evacuated tonight. They hope to bring out the guns and burn the bridges and ferry behind them. They will move straight to Lavaca and make a camp northwest of town. We are to shell the Union ships as long as we can and then retreat to Lavaca." Looking sadly at Otto, he continues, "After all that effort and expense to build the fort! Esperanza was a prophetic name."

They move into Indianola and locate the two guns on Water Street, just back from the water's edge in the business district. There they wait. Otto finds the waiting to be the worst part of this endeavor. His anguish rises steadily. Standing beside Reuss, he interrupts the quiet with a growl, "Damn them! They have completely changed our lives, and now they play with us like a cat with a mouse."

"Otto, your comparison is very apt. Maybe they intend to frighten us by prolonging the suspense." This is said with a smile, but underneath, Reuss's patience is wearing thin too.

* * *

Two days later, on October 31, the Union steamer *Westfield,* under the command of William B. Renshaw, accompanied by an armed schooner and a gunboat, steams past the abandoned Fort Esperanza and anchor off Indianola. Under a flag of truce, Captain Renshaw is rowed to the large wharf, where he is met by Shea and two Indianola businessmen. He makes himself perfectly clear. "I do not intend to occupy the town, but I will control the bay. I need supplies, particularly beef. I'll pay a reasonable price. If I can't buy it, I'll take it by force of arms."

When this statement is complete, the businessmen say they will not sell to the Union. Shea adds, "I will defend this place to the best of my ability."

Faced with this rejection, Renshaw says, "I will give you one hour to evacuate women and children, and then I shall bombard this town." Turning on his heel, he steps into his boat and returns under the white flag to the *Westfield.* An hour later, the white flag is lowered, and the bombardment begins.

It is a terribly one-sided engagement. Renshaw has fifteen guns on the ships anchored out in the bay, and Shea has only the two twelve-pounders. They exchange shots for over an hour with only minor damage to the Union ships and three casualties to Otto's gun crews. The wharves and warehouses are heavily damaged. Structures in the business district were riddled with shrapnel. Shea orders the two guns to Lavaca.

Otto walks through the ruins of Henry Runge's store on the way to order up the mule teams. There in the dirt is the $39.50 gingham dress. It has a long shrapnel-induced rip in the bodice. He thinks what an ironic end to the cotton that has been run through the Union blockade for the Union mills then run back through the blockade only to be destroyed by a Union ship. Turning abruptly, he chides himself for the luxury of ironic thoughts. He has a job to do getting his men and guns out of this mess and on to Lavaca.

* * *

Otto leaves the body of one man with his family and withdraws with two wounded in a wagon tended by Reuss. When they are well under way, he stops and gets into the wagon to check on their progress. Reuss is bent over one of the men who has a wound covered by a cotton wad painted with iodine and pressed tightly to his chest. His open shirt is soaked with bright-red blood. His face has turned a ghastly gray-white. Reuss looks up at Otto's questioning face and says, "I couldn't leave him in the care of his family. I don't know how the Union will treat wounded defenders." His voice trails off. Brightening, he indicates the man with a shrapnel wound on the side of his right thigh. "This fellow will do fine. He'll be dancing a *schottische* with a pretty girl in three months. I'll stick with them for a while."

Otto nods and drops off the wagon to remount his mule and continues the ride to Lavaca. He feels a deep sadness; these were not just men of his company but also his neighbors, men he had sung with and shared a jug of beer. The mule mirrors his sorrow with its head hanging low and its slow steps kicking dust on the road to Lavaca.

Chapter Twelve

When they are two miles from Lavaca, Vernon asks Otto to search the town and pick a site for emplacing the guns. The guns and men will wait for him behind Chocolate Bayou just south of town.

Taking Will Moore, Otto rides to the wharf at Lavaca. His immediate reaction is that there could hardly be a worse location for the guns. A low beach extends from the business district for perhaps fifty yards and offers no way to emplace the guns. With a shake of his head, he says, "Will, if we set the guns both here, the artillery and the business buildings will be a single target, and the inner harbor will provide room for the ships to position themselves. This would be a repetition of Indianola, where the ships could choose their targets, guns or businesses, with only a slight change in pointing."

Will frowns before saying, "Also, there's plenty of water in the inner harbor. They could anchor anywhere. If they put out multiple anchors, they could change the ship's position just by hauling in the right anchor line. We should do as much damage as we can to them before they get in here."

Thinking blackly on this, they ride southward; and there on a slight mound at the northeast corner of Chocolate Bayou, Otto's spirits rise. "Will, here's the place! There is enough dirt for a slight emplacement of the guns, and the narrow entrance to the inner harbor is directly ahead."

Will commented, "The gunboats could probably get through as there is six feet of water at the entrance to the harbor, but it's a narrow channel. The guns could fire at the ships approaching that entrance. The ships would be heading past us, unable to bring their main guns to bear." Turning the mules, they trot quickly to meet the column and direct them to this spot.

The crews are led to the promising spot. Otto, pointing, says to John Noll, "Dig pits for the two guns with a mound of dirt thrown up on each side and a low berm in front. Get lumber from the town to place under the wheels of the gun carriages."

"Otto, I can see that this will be a different situation and not just a replay of Indianola."

Otto is smiling as his spirits lift, saying, "Make a shielded spot nearby for the caissons. Unhitch the mules and move them well back from the gun position."

John and the crews fall to work immediately, sensing that they would have some protection of their own devising at this spot.

The larger guns from the evacuated fort pass behind them. A messenger confirms that they are out of ammunition. A wagon train is dispatched to Victoria for additional ammunition. Otto's confidence rises when he considers that their source of supplies is now only twelve miles away and over a good road not subject to enemy bombardment.

When the emplacement of the guns is complete, everyone settles in to wait. It is a long wait indeed. Two days pass. Again, Otto's anger rises as the time slowly passes, leaving him with nothing to do. He walks over to Reuss's location just to have something to do. Reuss confirms over a cup of corn coffee that the man with the chest wound had died during the first night, saying, "I lost that round with death. There is never much hope for a man with a punctured lung bleeding internally. The other fellow with the leg wound is doing quite well. It's remarkable to an oldster like me how quickly these youngsters can recover from injury. I've found a home here in Lavaca to take him in and care for him until we get settled someplace. It's well back from the waterfront, so maybe it will be safe from the bombardment." They both settle in to wait for the Yankees.

* * *

Finally, on the morning of October 31, two Union ships are seen steaming up the bay under a flag of truce. A truce boat is sent out to halt them before they could enter the inner harbor. They come to anchor at the mouth of the narrow channel and are met by Shea and four businessmen from Lavaca. Captain Renshaw, the Union officer, stands stiffly, saying, "I demand the surrender of this town."

Shea, remembering the bombast of Kittredge, steps into the captain's personal space, rises on his toes, and looking steadily at him, replies, "I am here to defend it and will do so to the best of my ability and with all the forces at my command." The Union officer steps back and addresses the businessmen, asking if they will sell him supplies. They assure him they will not. Chagrined at this affront, he stands for a moment in silence then, in an effort to be gentlemanly, replies, "Because there is a yellow fever epidemic here, I will give you one hour and a half to evacuate the town." With finality, he turns and steps into his boat to return to the ship.

Promptly an hour and a half later, the ships raise anchor, drop their white flags, and make to enter the inner harbor. Instantly, when the flag drops, the two twelve-pounders under the command of Reuss and Schnaubert fire. Otto watches the fall of the first shot and corrects the pointing. The next shot hits on board the leading ship, which continues its progress toward the inner bay. Otto orders a change to shot with contact fuses and elevates the gun slightly. On the command of "fire," he sees the shot land on the foredeck with a bright-red burst. A jib flaps freely as its sheet is severed and the ships head falls off to windward. This causes Reuss's next shot, a solid, to strike the starboard side forward just above the waterline. The ship drops all sails to regain control and avoid submerging the gaping shot holes in the bow. On steam alone, it maneuvers to the inner harbor, continuing to receive shots from the Confederate guns. Then it anchors with its forward gun aimed at the city. Will taps Otto on the arm, saying, "He's positioned to bombard the city. He has only one anchor forward and one aft. He can't easily shift his position and bring his guns around to bear on us."

Otto raises his field glasses and confirms that indeed he has an advantage on this ship. He shouts, "Load with solids." He aims for the waterline at the foremast. The shell hits a foot above the waterline. Now the ship is holed on both port and starboard sides close to the waterline. It dares not sail on a tack to either side but only steam downwind.

His attention turns to the other ship, the *Westfield,* which is now maneuvering into the inner bay. Otto and Reuss both begin to fire at the *Westfield,* which is moving more rapidly than the first ship and comes to anchor with only minor hits. Both ships begin to fire on the Lavaca business district and wharves. They are well situated to do this but cannot bring their main guns to bear on the two twelve-pounders.

The two twelve-pounders fire steadily during the day. They score hits on the Union ship's rigging and deckhouses. The lead ship is seriously damaged and withdraws. The *Westfield* continues firing until darkness, aiming chiefly at the town of Lavaca, which receives a total of 174 shot and shell that day. Only small pivot guns are fired at the Confederate cannons.

Otto is relieved to find that he has no casualties among the men and only two slight injuries among the mules. His sense of accomplishment soars. However, the town of Lavaca is thoroughly damaged with the business section nearly destroyed. The pride of the businessmen, who refused to trade with the Yankees, has been costly.

* * *

Reuss examines the 204 artillery men and finds twelve that were sufficiently advanced in yellow fever to require hospitalization. He comments to Otto, "This is a problem. We've got to get them indoors out of the weather, but anywhere in the town, they will be shelled tomorrow."

Vernon walks up to get a report on the day's action. Reuss presents him with the problem. Vernon lowers his head, tugs at his moustache for a moment, and then replies, "When we left the fort, I had the rain catchments taken off the cisterns and packed into wagons. They're over on Agua Dulce Creek. We could use some of the lumber from these broken buildings and make a sort of lean-to like an Indian teepee covered with the canvas of the catchment, leaving a hole at the top for ventilation. That would permit a small fire inside, and the troops could be kept warm in a single place."

Reuss allows that will work fine, saying, "I'll detail some men to move the lumber and slowly walk the sick men to the creek." It proved to be a long walk, and by the time Reuss and the men arrive, the lean-to is finished and a fire is burning inside. The men are bedded down on folded canvas tents covered with blankets. Reuss says, "This is as good as can be done. We'll see how they are in the morning."

* * *

On the following day, the *Westfield* returns alone, firing on the town for a total of seventy-four rounds before leaving in the afternoon. The two twelve-pounders continued to fire as long as the ship is within range.

The two artillery batteries are served coffee, bread, and meat during the firing on both days by remarkably brave ladies of Lavaca. The engagement is viewed locally as a significant Confederate victory in which the Union ships were defeated and forced to flee. In fact, they did flee Lavaca but returned to Indianola, where they discharged soldiers that occupied the city.

* * *

A detachment of Breckenridge's cavalry rides to Indianola that night to observe the occupation. It returns just before dawn and reports that all of the infantry are located in the city and the ship is tied up at the wharves. Shea thinks this will determine the battle line for the winter with the Union in Indianola and the Confederates in Lavaca. He ventures, "Twelve miles of flat, treeless land between the forces means that neither can mount an attack without great and prolonged exposure to the artillery fire of the other. It's a stalemate." On the following day, a norther blows in and precludes any movement by either side.

The lean-to hospital serves well, and Shea's battalion makes camp near Clark Station on the railway northwest of town. There is fresh water for soldiers and mules from Agua Dulce Creek and excellent rye grass for the mules' forage. There is even some wood to feed the cooking fires and the one that warms the lean-to. Commissary supplies are available from Lavaca and Victoria. When the cold, wet wind of the norther stops, preparations are made to spend the winter.

Bletchley's company moves to Victoria, and John Ireland's infantry company moves from Victoria to join Shea's battalion. This is uniformly viewed as a positive development. Bletchley is not missed, and Ireland, who captured Union captain Kittredge, is a welcome addition. Reuss wonders to himself, *How did Shea accomplish that? I knew it was going to happen, but I never saw him turn a hair.*

* * *

Christmas approaches. The differences between their present situation at the Lavaca encampment and that of the preceding year at Fort Esperanza become evident to all and a concern to the senior officers. The size of the battalion has increased from 304 to over 400. Their efforts have made the position as strong as a temporary bivouac could be. Food, grass, water, and firewood are plentiful. There is no sight of the enemy except by the cavalry patrols. In short, boredom is setting in. Morale, which had been high following the successful duel with the Union ships at Lavaca, is beginning to fade.

It is Lt. Christian French, the party planner, the one negotiating the trade of oysters for champagne the preceding Christmas, who comes up with a promising idea. He speaks to the senior officers' mess, "Gentlemen, we are suffering from our own success. The men are comfortable and completely lacking a challenge."

"What do you suggest, Chris?" asks Shea.

The immediate reply is "We do our cooking on a company basis, how about a contest among the four companies for the best Christmas dinner?" This is greeted by a stunned silence from the senior officers who are well aware of the problem but were thinking of solutions in military terms. Their position and the Yankee strength simply did not allow any initiatives from the Confederates; hence, their thinking had produced no solution.

"What the men need is a challenge, and we can generate that within our own camp." Shea moves forward, resting his elbows on the table and his chin in his hands. Chris continues, "Each dinner will be prepared and served for the entire company. A team of judges comprising Major Shea, two businessmen from Lavaca, and the four company commanders will sample the dinners at each company mess and then vote on the winner. Each company will be allowed to develop its own menu from whatever it could obtain by requisition, hunting, fishing, or purchase by collection not to exceed twenty dollars. But it must feed all members of the company as well as the judges." This is at first greeted by a continuing silence. One by one, the senior officers begin to relax and smile.

"My god, Chris, you may have something," says Reuss. Shea sits back in his chair and looks from one to another of the officers and sees beginning acceptance.

"What would be the prize?" asks Shea.

"It would be a barrel of beer if I could get to my store in Indianola, but that's out of the question. I've talked this over with Otto," he says, glancing at Schnaubert. "He has agreed that six musicians from his company would form a brass sextet and play Christmas music at supper that evening for the winning company."

"I've got only one thing to add," says Shea. "The officers will dine with their companies that day and pay a nominal fee for the privilege." There is a moment of silence and then a burst of unanimous applause.

*   *   *

The competition catches on immediately. Planning meetings take place with sentries posted around each conference tent to guard against spies from the other companies. Ideas become so grandiose that additional rules are necessary. Each company is limited to only one wagon and four mules for transporting supplies. No more than ten men from a company could leave the area during the day and none at night.

Breckenridge's cavalry has some advantage in the distance it could cover under the rules. The Indianola companies feel they were at a disadvantage because they are denied by the Union from the area that they know best, the lower bay and the islands. Ireland's infantry company simply keeps quiet. They have a double threat. The original members include many Germans from New Braunfels and the Hill Country, which have a distinctly different idea of food preparation. The later members came from the coastal regions and are well versed in seafood preparation.

*   *   *

On Christmas Eve Day, the judges make their rounds then cast their votes. Each judge can give five points for originality and five points for "good eatin'." There is much discussion, but the final count shows Ireland's men the winners. They used most of their collection to buy four sheep, and the company turned out in force, using the offal from the sheep to catch crabs in the bayous. They served fried crab cakes and barbecued mutton with rice and red beans, buttermilk biscuits, and pecan pie.

Breckenridge's cavalry company is second, having used their horses to scout in depth until they found a farmer with the right-sized hog that he was willing to slaughter, scald, and pick out the hair, chill overnight, and deliver for eight cents a pound. They constructed a spit with drip pans and, over a fire pit, roasted the pig all day. It was served whole with a yam in its mouth accompanied by sweet potatoes, rice and red beans, crusty white bread, and pecan pie.

Otto's artillery felt they were at a disadvantage, as their favorite source of food, the lower bay, was not available with Indianola occupied. They did what they could with seafood from the upper bay. However, they were in third place, serving chowder made with croakers and gafftop catfish followed by roast beef, red beans, white bread, and sweet potato pie.

Vernon's artillery had the same problems as Otto's company and followed closely with roast beef, sweet potatoes, white bread, and sugar cookies.

Ireland's company agrees to eat supper one hour late and invites the others to sit nearby and enjoy the music of the brass sextet, which gained much credit for the performance. Later that evening, a single trumpet played "Stillege Nacht, Heillege Nacht" in the cold night air. It is heard by the pickets and cavalry patrol at their lonely posts in the treeless coastal prairie. Many eyes are damp as thoughts turn to the beautiful forests of southern Germany, far away in both time and distance.

Part IV

CHAPTER THIRTEEN

January 1863

Major Vernon presided at the senior officers' mess in a tent at the Lavaca encampment. His face bore a huge smile that broadened his heavy black mustache. He addresses the assembled group, "Gentlemen, there is truly a heap of good news tonight." There is a rustling at the table. All heads turn to him. There were rumors all afternoon, and now they would hear the true story. Vernon continues, "I have the Houston paper, just brought in on horseback. You can read the story later. Basically, General Magruder has captured Galveston through a brilliant combined operation of naval and land forces." This confirmation of the rumor brings out a huge cheer.

When the noise subsides, Vernon continues, "We have captured the large cruiser, *Harriet Lane.* Also, there's good news for us especially. The *Westfield* has exploded and sunk, with Captain Renshaw killed." This latter news prompts a second cheer in a normally restrained group. The man who ordered the shelling of Indianola and Lavaca and his hated ship are no more.

Motioning for attention, Vernon continues, "The entire Union garrison, quartered in a single warehouse riddled by artillery shells, finally surrendered to an infantry battalion. The Union artillery at the east end of Galveston Island, left without defense, was captured intact. A great amount of Union stores were captured undamaged. Incredibly, Confederate casualties were very light."

Everyone gathers around Vernon to get a look at the paper, which features an engraving of the *Harriet Lane* speared by the bow of the *Bayou City.* Individual discussions break out until Vernon prompts all to be seated and discuss the matter over dinner. Seated at the head of the table, he breaks a slice of cornbread and asks, "What do you gentlemen think this means for us?" There is a brief silence, then Captain Ireland, commander of the infantry, brings his lawyerly analysis and fine tactical sense to bear. He ventures, "The loss of Galveston is a major blow to the Union. Old Farragut must be turning purple right now. I expect this means any invasion of central Texas is taken off the plans. Their idea was to join up forces between here and Galveston, but with Galveston in our hands, that won't work."

Turning to Ireland, Vernon questions, "Do you think they will pull out of fort Esperanza?"

Ireland finishes chewing a tough piece of beef and says, "I don't know, but if I were in Farragut's shoes, I'd give up on the central coast and try to stop both sea and land traffic with Mexico in the vicinity of Brownsville. That would mean Fort Esperanza would be of no importance to me."

This statement causes a thoughtful silence at the table, each person asking what that would mean to them if the fort were to be reoccupied. Vernon interrupts their thoughts. "It's not all good news. Captain Reuss was captured while on a visit to one of his patients in Indianola. Because he's a doctor and his service is needed in town, the Yankees paroled him with the requirement that he report to the Union commander every morning." Eyebrows were raised, and individual thoughts turn to the possible result of this news. Vernon continues, "Assistant Surgeon George Jones will oversee the hospital. I'm promoting Otto Schnaubert to be the commander of Reuss's company, and Otto Beyer will be his first lieutenant." Congratulations and handshakes descend onto both Ottos. Individual conversations broke out concerning this overload of news. The talk continues over the smoke from pipes loaded with crumbled grapevine bark. It is a long time before sleep claims the officers of Shea's battalion.

* * *

Ireland's prognosis proved to be surprisingly accurate. Indianola is abandoned by the Union after a month, and shortly thereafter, the troops occupying Fort Esperanza withdraw. This proved to be a further catastrophe to the city of Indianola as extensive looting accompanied the withdrawal. Reuss, with no place to report, begins to make periodic visits to the encampment but honors his parole by wearing mufti instead of his uniform.

In February, Shea's battalion is incorporated into the Eighth Texas Infantry with the two artillery units becoming companies A and B. This regiment is commanded by Colonel A. M. Hobby. Shea becomes a lieutenant colonel and is given responsibility for the coastal defenses from Cedar Bayou to Velasco with Hobby responsible from Cedar Bayou south. Both Shea and Hobby report to a Colonel W. R. Bradfute.

The battalion remains at Lavaca during the spring of 1863. The mules fatten on a new crop of rye grass and the fresh water of Agua Dulce Creek. The higher command in Houston debates the best use of the troops, with indecision being the main product.

* * *

In May 1863, the battalion reoccupies Fort Esperanza. After the guns are ashore, a conference of officers meets in the bombproof dugout, with Shea presiding. The room appears much the worse after the Yankee abandonment and four months of neglect. His first question is to Vernon. "What is the status of the battalion?"

To Vernon, this was like old times, but his answer displays the difference. "We have 504 men, 202 from the two artillery companies, 79 cavalry, and 221 infantry from various units of the Eighth Texas. All are present here at the fort."

Shea continues, "And the water supply?"

"We have about twenty days' supply in the cisterns. The men are rigging the canvas catchments. I've sent a party over to Saluria to determine what water is there."

"What about ordnance, Otto?"

"We have seven twenty-four-pounders, one 128-pounder, and two twelve-pounders. They are being emplaced now. We are in good shape for ammunition with one hundred rounds for the 128-pounder and about two hundred rounds for each of the others. Powder is adequate."

"And supplies, Beyer?"

"We are in good shape with forty days' supply of corn and beans. There's an equal supply of forage for the horses and mules. However, I suggest that we move half of the mules ashore to reduce the demand on the water supply."

"Captain Ireland, have you had a chance to survey the trench system?"

"That's being done right now. What I could see of it is in poor shape, but we will have crews on it today."

"Captain Breckenridge, how is your cavalry?"

"We are still surveying the island. My first reaction is that we should quarter our company in Saluria, where we could go ashore or come back to the island as the need develops."

"Does anyone have anything to add?" There is no reply, so he continues, "Otto, place two lookouts at the lighthouse. Have them show one flag if Yankees are on land and two if they are at sea. Just like Paul Revere. Also, put the twelve-pounders, one at Saluria and one with the troops down the island. Ireland, as soon as your men can occupy the trenches, put out pickets a mile and a half down the island. Have them watch the top of the lighthouse for a flag warning."

He surveys the faces to see if there was any doubt or questions. Finding none, he continues, "Ireland, I'd like for you to maintain two patrols down the island, one on the bay side and one on the Gulf side, to watch for any Union troops or boats. In addition, there should be four mounted dispatch riders here at headquarters on a twenty-four-hour basis. Any questions?" There are none.

* * *

The marriage of Frances Dickerson and Will Moore is the social event of the summer, partly because of the popularity of the two as individuals and partly because of the management of Erdmuthe Thompson, Frances's mother. She had married three times and brought a connoisseur's eye and a gracious hand to the planning. Her first marriage was to Adolph Weisenberg in Germany. They brought Frances and Adolph Jr. to Texas in 1851. Adolph Sr. died of yellow fever shortly after they landed. Erdmuthe, or "Mutti" as she came to be called, was a widow for less than a year. She and Charles Dickerson were married in Indianola, and Frances chose to change her name to Dickerson. Adolph did not and continued as a Weisenberg. Mutti again became a widow in 1858 with the death of Charles.

They had a son, Charles Jr., in 1858. He would later marry Lina Katlyn. Again, Mutti was a widow for less than a year when she married Robert Thompson. Her outstanding attribute was care for others. When she spoke to anyone, they felt as if there was no one else in all of creation. They had the total attention of this woman. Naturally, this had a profound effect on men and largely explains the brevity of her widowhoods.

Her planning for the wedding begins with the question to herself, "How can I overcome the shortages of food that the blockade imposes?" The answer takes a while but clearly orders, "Concentrate on other things." She lists in her head those other things. First, the regimental band is almost all drawn from Otto's company, as is Will. A little persuasion on Otto through Mary results in seventy-two-hour passes for six musicians who are pleased to play at the reception in the church's meeting room after the wedding.

Mary herself, six months pregnant with her first son, sews a dress, which drapes from her bust line and makes a comfortable and elegant appearance. Mutti, asking what the baby would be named, is advised, "Charles if it's a boy or Mary if it's a girl. And you are going to be godmother."

"Father" Orr is actually a Methodist but shares his church building with the towns Catholics and so earned the name "Father." He is happy to officiate as he had at the wedding of Otto and Mary.

Mutti hung around the post office until she saw one of the older men of the town, who had formed a men's singing group in years before the war. Smiling warmly, she says, "Hans, you men have not sung together in three years, not since the last big *Sangerfest* in San Antonio. Do you suppose that you could get together and sing at the wedding of Frances and Will Moore?" Hans thinks about this for a moment and then says he would get together all of the men he could find. He did, and they found tears in their eyes as they practiced old world favorites to sing at the wedding and the reception. Henry Runge, under Mutti's encouragement, donates a keg of beer to lubricate the singers. Lieutenants George and Christian French donate four bottles of schnapps from their liquor store. Mutti herself provides a large mound of peach fritters for the ladies. The aroma fills the reception area and complements the scent of wild flowers arranged in canning jars set on the tables. The affair is a huge success. Music is heard long after the couple retired to a donated room at the one hotel still open in town.

* * *

The high spirits do not last. In mid-July, the Houston newspapers bring word of the Vicksburg surrender. Henry Runge stands in front of his store with the paper in hand. He gestures to the first citizen passing by, saying, "This will have more effect on us than is at first apparent. It closes the Mississippi River as a route for us to transfer goods, supplies, ammunition, and troops. Indianola, with its greatly reduced flow of goods, will see trade drop to zero." The citizen who still had dreams of Indianola becoming a highway of commerce mourns in sympathy. A week later comes the news of Lee's defeat at Gettysburg. Although this brings great anguish to the Eastern Confederate states, to the citizens of Indianola, it seems the lesser of the two events.

That summer brings the birth of Charles Schnaubert to Mary and Otto. With no immediate pressure on the fort, Otto is able to be with Mary the day following the birth and see his son. Turning to Mutti, who had helped with the birth, he asks, "Is it all right that his face is so red?" He is assured by Mutti, Frances Moore, and Mrs. Reuss that indeed this is normal and would clear in a day or so. Mary takes the baby, whom everyone begins to call "Charly," from Mutti and starts to nurse him. This time, Otto is slowly aroused from his thoughts about his heir and turned to the future together with Mary.

* * *

A written order from Shea requires two men to be assigned temporarily on the supply ship that transports material to refurbish the fort. Vernon places this order on Otto, saying, "Your company has more mariners than the rest of us, being as you're all from a port city. Take care of this." Otto does, detailing two of his men with maritime experience, Williams and Wilkerson. Later that afternoon, John Noll, facing Otto with a stern face, says, "Captain Schnaubert, these men refuse to go aboard the ship."

"Bring them to me." John produces the two men, whom Otto addresses, "Men, you are ordered to serve temporarily aboard the supply ship loading and unloading material required here at the fort. You will take your orders from the ship's captain until I relieve you for service here."

This produces a shuffling of feet, then Williams stands straight, saying, "Captain Schnaubert, we cannot board that ship."

Otto's stern look shifts to Wilkerson, who says, "I can't board either."

Otto is horrified. Four years in the U.S. Army gives him a lurid picture of where this was leading. They were in the presence of the enemy cruising the Gulf just out of range. These men are refusing to obey a direct order. Again, he addresses the men, "Do you realize the seriousness of what you are doing? If you insist on disobeying my order, the result will be a court-martial. The outcome may be your execution. Do you understand?"

Williams again took the lead, "Yes, sir, but if we go on that boat, we will die for sure. There's yellow fever aboard her. We'll take our chances with the court-martial instead of a sure death on board that ship."

Otto looks them directly in the eyes for a long two minutes in silence and then says, "All right, you are under arrest. I'll prefer charges this afternoon. Come with Sergeant Noll and me to the guardhouse." The men are securely locked in, and Otto goes to find Reuss. With the Yankees at a comfortable distance, Dr. Reuss was easy to find in the fort's hospital dressed in mufti and doing rounds with fifteen yellow fever patients.

"Reuss, I've got to talk with you as soon as possible. I've got a terrible problem."

"Walk around to the officers' mess. I'll be there in fifteen minutes" was his reply. In exactly fifteen minutes, Reuss enters, saying, "From the looks of you, Otto, the problem isn't your health. What is it?"

"I have a terrible dilemma. You see, two of my men have refused a direct order to go on board the supply ship because they think they'll die of yellow fever. That fear isn't ridiculous. Two of the ships crewmen died of yellow fever this past week. I have no choice but to order charges against them, and there'll be a court-martial. They will likely be shot. Now I have to order two more men to go aboard. If I don't, I'll face a court-martial. If I do, I may be sending them to die needlessly of yellow fever."

"As your doctor, I'm prescribing two fingers of grain alcohol, partly to calm you down but mainly to give me time to think about this." He ducks around the corner to his medical supplies chest and returns immediately, filling a glass at the counter in the mess. "That's 180 proof medical alcohol. No one will detect an odor on you. Now about that problem." He settles back in a chair and begins a monologue, "The medical profession doesn't know what causes yellow fever. I've seen a lot of it and can tell you one thing—it's not contagious. I work all the time with sick and dying patients. Nurses do too. I've never caught it." He paused, looking thoughtful.

"Somehow, it has to do with water and warm weather. But you know—strange thing—it's more active at night. I've seen nurses work on night shift in a hospital with yellow fever patients and have no problems. Of course, the hospital has mosquito bars and is real clean. Then they shift to working days and going home at night, where they might not have the protection of the hospital, and they catch yellow fever." He pulls out a pipe and begins loading it from his tiny supply of tobacco. "It seems to require a source of standing water. I've drained ponds and had good results. But I don't subscribe to that 'miasma rising from the water' theory. I've never seen a miasma."

"Let me suggest something. Suppose I go on board that ship during the daytime and see if there isn't a lot of water in the bilges. If there is, we'll pump them dry. Then we will arrange for your men to work aboard only during the daytime and sleep here in the hospital at night, just like the nurses that worked nights. The captain can arrange his schedule to do that. I think that will protect your men quite well. What do you say?"

Otto thinks on it. Yes, he can live with that. He will have protected his men as best he could on medical advice. His stomach muscles begin to relax. Then smiling at Reuss, he says, "That's good advice. Can we go down and look at the ship now?" They did and found the bilges standing with eight inches of water, mainly from rain rather than leakage in the hull. The bilges are pumped and then swept down to remove the trash that had accumulated there. The captain agrees to a schedule placing him at the fort each evening and pumping the bilges each morning.

Armed with this preparation, Otto speaks to his officers and sergeants and explains the precautions. He then asks them for recommendations on men who are in very good health. This is discussed at length, and each sergeant is asked to recommend one man from his unit. The following day, Otto addresses the recommended men. I need two volunteers for a special task that will take you away from the fort during the day but back each evening. In the evening, you'll sleep in the hospital here with mosquito bars for your beds." There are four volunteers. Otto picks two, explaining the precautions in Reuss's recommendations. He outlines the mission. There is no objection. A break from camp routine is always welcome, and there is great respect for Reuss's medical opinion.

Otto prepares the charges for Williams and Wilkerson. Vernon recommends a court-martial. The papers go to Shea in Indianola. He does not act on them. As the fall days pass and the yellow fever epidemic subsides, Vernon simply cancels the recommendation and has Williams and Wilkerson released. As he says to Otto, "A commander can, at his own discretion, waive a court-martial after ninety days if, in his view, that is the best course of action. I anticipate that we will have a fight with the Yankees very shortly, and we will need all our men." The volunteers survive the season having no problem from yellow fever with Reuss's cleansed boat and indoor-sleeping routine.

* * *

Frances Moore moves in with Mary Schnaubert and her two children. Both the Moores and the Schnauberts are on the Calhoun County list of indigent families. These are chiefly the homes of Confederate soldiers' wives who found it difficult to make ends meet with their husbands away. The county imposes a property tax of fifty cents per hundred dollars of evaluation, and from this pay, the families receive fifty dollars per year for each adult and twenty-five dollars for each child. With this $150 per year, Frances and Mary pay the rent on their house. They take in sewing to cover the cost of food.

Sitting one day at the kitchen table, Mary and Frances sew while Lina plays on the floor and Charly lies in the crib. Finishing the hem of a dress, Frances says, "I am frightened about Will. He is so confident of himself that he takes on any risk. I know he's strong and he's real bright, but he does not know how to be afraid."

Mary looks up from her work, asking, “What has he done that worries you?”

“You know when Major Shea got permission to put guns on two small ships to make a Confederate navy inside the bay? Will was the first to volunteer to serve aboard them. Naturally they took him. He was one of the few that knew how to manage a ship and also serve a cannon.”

Mary gets up to lay a stick of wood on the fire of the kitchen stove, which is the heating means for the whole house. Sitting, she asks, “Well, is that especially dangerous?”

“He’s on the *Carr,* which, along with the *Cora,* is all that we have. The Union has dozens of ships here and outside Galveston. Will says they’re too big to get in the bay, but if they bring some smaller ones in, he will defend the upper end of the bay and the rivers that empty into it. They’re letting him take the duties of second mate on the *Carr,* and with his self-confidence, I’m afraid of the chances he might take.”

Mary, remembering all that Otto had said about Will, responds, “Don’t poor-mouth him. Otto always spoke highly of him, said he is very observant and has a cool head in action. He always took Will with him if there was any question about the Union ships.”

“Will holds Otto in the highest regard. I think he sees him as a hero and tries to be like him. He thought Otto is the best artillerist that the Confederacy has in Texas. You know Will wants to command his own ship one day. He admires the way Otto takes care of his men and says he learned a lot about command by watching him.”

“All right, Frances, our husbands like and admire each other, and we love ’em to death. But they will be themselves. Aren’t we lucky?”

CHAPTER FOURTEEN

November 1863

In the summer of 1863, events well removed from Indianola conspire to produce a profound effect on Fort Esperanza. Maj. General Halleck, commanding the Union Trans-Mississippi Army, has a preconception not shared by many of his colleagues. He sees the ascendancy of Napoleon III in Mexico as an attempt by France to reestablish itself on the North American continent. In his view, Mexico will attack and occupy Texas, while Texans are occupied fighting for the Confederacy in the East. The clear solution in his mind is to invade Texas with Union troops. France will think twice before attacking America, whereas attacking a seceded Texas is a small concern.

Halleck sets three forces in motion under the command of Napoleon P. T. Banks. One will capture Brownsville, on the border with Mexico, and hold it and the Rio Grande River. A second will attempt to invade Texas directly from Louisiana. A third will invade from the Gulf, controlling the rivers of central Texas and linking up with the others. On the Confederate side, General Magruder anticipates these three and imagines a fourth from the north.

* * *

The talk in the officers' mess at Fort Esperanza turns on the tremendous success of the Confederate forces at the Sabine River in stopping the Yankee invasion of Texas. Vernon, taking the lead, says, "It's a great example of what our artillery can do. They were drilled to a fare-thee-well by their captain, and when he became ill, an Irish saloon keeper takes over. He captures two Union ships, thirteen guns, and 350 prisoners."

This prompts Christian French, Indianola's saloon keeper, to say, "You should be more gracious in the presence of your honored saloon keepers."

"And their brothers" comes from George French. A roar of laughter is the reply. It is the first major victory in Texas since the capture of Galveston.

* * *

Beyer joins in the laughter. Later that night, he and Otto walk to their tent, where Beyer moved when Reuss was captured. He raises the question, "So what does that mean for us here?"

"Well, Beyer, you have a way of putting your finger on the key item in a barrel full of questions. I'd say it's not really good news for us. The Yankees are determined to invade Texas. If they did not succeed at the Sabine, they'll try again some other place. I doubt that they are ready for Galveston, so we are probably high on the list."

Otto's view is shared by General Magruder, who is in charge of the entire force in Texas. His problem is that the war in Louisiana siphoned off most of his reserves. So while all Texas celebrates the Sabine victory, he moves his meager forces to protect Matagorda Bay. Infantry is added at Fort Esperanza and Cavalry at Saluria.

* * *

It is November 18, nine o'clock in the evening. For once, the wind stops. Before the fog rolls in, the sky is a marvelous black with stars glittering like diamonds. Otto stands outside his tent, gazing in the direction of Indianola. He locates Polaris, the North Star, well known to all surveyors. In his head, he drops a plumb line through Polaris. At the horizon, it passes right through the house where Mary, Lina, and little Charly live. Frances Moore moved in after her wedding to Will. What a treasure that little house holds. He wonders if it's a sinful thought to compare Polaris and his Mary to the star of Bethlehem and the other Mary? Maybe God will understand. A man can grow lonely so near and yet so far from his family.

His attention is pulled back to earth as the sound of running steps invade the nighttime quiet. A man approaches and, saluting, yells, "Mr. Schnaubert! Mr. Beyer!"

"Yes, I'm Schnaubert."

"Sir, Major Ireland wants all junior officers and troops at their action stations, all senior officers in headquarters immediately."

Otto returns the salute and yells, "Beyer, all men and officers to action stations. Join me in headquarters as soon as action stations are set. Before you ask, I don't know why."

Otto retrieves his cap and gloves from the tent, starting for the dugout. He enters, seeing Major Ireland, now commander of the fort, standing in front of a map of Matagorda Bay and Aransas Bay nailed to the wall of the room. There is a distinct frown on his face. Colonel Bradfute stands next to him but seems content to leave the conduct of the meeting up to the fort's commander.

When all the first lieutenants complete the readying of the fort and enter the room, Ireland says, "Gentlemen, I have very bad news. You recall the company-strength infantry unit that we had on Mustang Island? They performed well this summer in capturing a Yankee raiding force. Well, they have now been overcome themselves by a large Union force landing on the island. The Union has several transports loaded with infantry. They are now landing on St. Joseph Island. I fear it's just a matter of time before they are on Matagorda Island with us." The moment of silence breaks as the breath held in check by the men is suddenly exhaled. Ireland waits a few seconds then resumes.

"Colonel Bradfute escaped from Aransas by the steamer *Cora* and arrived tonight at Saluria. He has notified General Magruder and started preparations to protect Esperanza. There will be a regiment of cavalry moved to Matagorda so it can transfer by ship over to Saluria. We now have two companies of infantry and expect a third to move into the fort shortly."

Looking about the room and seeing rapt attention, he continues, "I am moving a force of two platoons from my company down the island ten miles as an advanced picket. Captain Schnaubert, I'd like one of your twelve-pounders to accompany that unit. The remainder of the infantry will be in the trenches here at the Fort. I'd like your other twelve-pounder at the dug-in position behind the trenches. Also, I want to know whether a second twenty-four-pounder can be moved to support the trenches and assist that one in the northwest corner. Look that over and report to me tomorrow morning. Major Vernon, please prepare for me a complete list of commissary and ordnance supplies at the fort also for tomorrow morning." Again he looked around the room. "Any questions?" There are none. "Good, dismissed."

* * *

Shortly after daybreak on November 27, Otto takes the telescope and changes places with one of the two lookouts at the lighthouse. This will be an ideal time to examine the west end of the island with the sun behind him. The clear weather still holds, but the wind is rising. That made the climb a sporting event as the lighthouse leans precariously after a failed attempt to destroy it with a powder charge at the base. The task had been carried out by Bletchley, who knew nothing of building structures or tearing them down. His sole accomplishment was to crack one of the cast-iron plates at the base. Otto cautions himself to forget Bletchley and concentrate on the examination of the island.

The sound of distant musket fire is heard over the wind noise as he steps onto the top platform. Training his telescope down the island, he focuses it and then quietly mutters, "Lieber Gott!" At a distance of ten miles, he can just see Union ships unloading infantry, which then form up on the shore. Taking a pad and pencil from his pocket, he hands it to the lookout. "Write down what I tell you. I want this to go to Major Ireland." The lookout takes the materials and then writes out:

November 27, 1863

At lighthouse. Visible at ten miles—seven regiments of Union troops unloaded. Advancing on pickets who fire and retreat. More troops unloading from transport vessels.

Captain O. L. Schnaubert

"Take my mule and deliver that immediately to Major Ireland. Send the other lookout up here." Turning, he watches a steady stream of troops come off the transport vessels. Looking closely, he finds two cannon being wheeled forward by men, not mules. The Confederate pickets continue to retreat among the sandhills, stop to reload, fire, and move on. The scattered firing is just audible atop the lighthouse. Otto reflects that it probably is not heard at the fort. His message will come as a complete surprise. He is correct.

Ireland, reading the message, grunts and says, "Is he drunk?" then recalls that he has never even seen Otto drinking, much less drunk. He yells, "Vernon, take over here. I've got to go to the lighthouse and find out what Schnaubert sees." Going outside, he relieves one of the mounted couriers of his horse and gallops off to the lighthouse.

* * *

Otto, watching the movements of the pickets, is surprised by the comment at his elbow, "What are you seeing?" He hands the telescope to an angry Ireland who carefully focuses it and mutters, "Good Lord!" Turning, he says, "I owe you an apology. I should have known that after four years in the U.S. Army, you could tell the difference between a company and a regiment. I make that to be about four thousand men at this point. The cannons are no good to them now against the pickets all scattered in the sandhills, but as they near the fort, that will change." Thinking for a moment, he continues, "I want you back at the fort. Send one of your best men down here as lookout and have him report every hour." With that, Ireland goes down the ladder, while Otto passes the telescope to the remaining lookout. Handing him the pad and pencil, he orders, "Write out an observation once an hour and send it to the fort. I'll have a man with a mule here to relieve you so you can act as courier."

* * *

Back at the fort, Otto locates John Noll, explains the situation, and sends him on to the lighthouse as lookout. With his head down in thought, he walks to the headquarters room where the senior officers are gathering. Ireland motions for silence and explains the situation as he has seen it at the lighthouse. "The fort has approximately five hundred men. There are about one thousand cavalry that will be assembled at Matagorda in two days to be sent to Saluria by transports already there. Two batteries of heavy artillery, about two hundred men, are being moved from Refugio and will be in Saluria in two days. Five companies of infantry in Victoria will also be forwarded to Saluria." Turning his head to survey the group, he continues, "I make that to be a maximum of two thousand men that we would have to face about four thousand Yankees. That will probably grow to 5,500 in the next two days. Please let me have your views of our best course of action."

Vernon begins, "We have looked at the possibility of moving any of the twenty-four-pounders that are facing Pass Cavallo over to cover the advance of the Union troops. I am sorry to say that this doesn't look feasible. The guns would be out in the open, mounted on loose sand, with no chance of emplacing them. They would simply be destroyed by the Union cannon, as ours moved slowly through the sand to achieve a good firing position. We will have to depend on the one gun in the fort that faces west. However, there is the prepared position on Bayucos Island close to Saluria. We could emplace one twenty-four-pounder there."

"Good, move the one gun to Bayoucos." Then surveying the room, he asks, "Opinions, Beyer?"

"Major Ireland, the problem seems to me to be the convergence of all our supporting forces at the main shore in two days. Everyone says they are going to Saluria, but they all have to go over to Saluria on the one ferry. That will be a terrible congestion." This flat statement brings on a chorus of grunts acknowledging the truth of the picture as each man imagines the terrible congestion at the Saluria ferry. Ireland motions for quiet, and Beyer continues, "The only force that can go directly to Saluria is the cavalry on the ships from Matagorda. They will require good weather to make that run. The wind has been rising all day. I think we have a norther coming. That will put the transport out of commission for three, maybe four days."

"Schnaubert?"

"I think Beyer is right about the congestion coming in. If we have to evacuate the fort, there will be a terrible congestion at the Saluria ferry going in the other direction. I calculate about fifteen hours to transport the men. The two small howitzers would take under an hour, but the nine main guns would require about five, maybe six hours."

"French?"

"Sir, if I put myself in the position of the Yankees, I see the fort with this mile and a half long chain of bridges and a ferry that communicate to the mainland. If I bombard the fort with my two cannons and send my cavalry in to interdict that chain, I've got the fort bottled up. Then it's a long bombardment followed by the attack of my 3,500 infantry against the five hundred at the fort. In short, it's just a matter of time."

Ireland walks back and forth twice in the silent room then stops and, looking up, says, "I'll speak for the infantry myself. We have three hundred men supported by two twelve-pounder howitzers. We would do well to hold out one day. Two days seem unlikely unless the enemy makes some stupid mistake." He stops and, surveying the room, sees that his men feel it is hopeless to hold out. He continues, "All right, I have to view the evacuation of the fort as the only course. Our effort should be to save all that we can for the Confederacy and deny the rest to the enemy. We shall begin preparations tonight. Vernon, I want your men to tear down these interior walls to make kindling for burning our commissary supplies and to fire the powder magazines. When we evacuate, you will set fire to the bridges. Your men will be the last to go out.

"Schnaubert, take your small howitzers and emplace them to enfilade the enemy's infantry as it approaches the fort. Also, at the last minute, you will personally spike the main guns. Tonight, I want you to load all wagons with supplies and powder and send them over to the main shore. When the main evacuation starts, you will be the first to go over with your two guns and emplace them on the main shore to fire over our evacuating troops and keep the enemy at bay. Do not use fused shells over the heads of our people, fuses are too unreliable. Use solids or contact plungers.

"I will direct the infantry. We will leave after Schnaubert and before Vernon." Then pausing, he asks, "Is all of that clear?" It was.

* * *

With heavy heart, Vernon directs the tearing down of the interior walls that were once siding of Confederate homes until they were wrecked by Yankees and then salvaged by Confederates. Now they will be burned by another group of Confederates to deny supplies to another group of Yankees. What insanity!

The wagons pass over the ferry the night of the twenty-seventh, pulled by the mules that would normally move the main guns. On the twenty-eighth, the Union forces are within one and a half miles of the fort, with the Union infantry occupying the outer trenches, and the Confederates the inner trenches of the fort's defensive system. The Union general commanding the Third Corps sits in a pit dug in a sandhill behind the Union infantry facing the fort. He is an active leader and has been with his troops all the way from the landing area. He sits with one of his colonels, a lieutenant from his staff, and a sergeant guard armed with a Sharps repeating rifle. Of the four, he is the best dressed to withstand the rising cold, wet wind. He wears a Union-issue heavy overcoat and wool cape, topped with a felt fisherman's hood. He lowers his field glasses, saying, "Damn them! They've got a large cannon into that emplacement on the island over by the ferry. Must have pulled it in last night. If I had my cavalry I'd capture it right now, but it would be hopeless to try it with infantry right under the eyes of the fort."

The colonel stirs, rubbing his cold hands together, and offers, "I don't know what idiot in New Orleans planned the ship loading. All the horses are on the deep-water transports that can't unload at the pass and can't get into the bay because of shallow water. We've got cavalrymen but no horses." In disgust, he spits on the sand and moves to cover it with his boot. The steady wind has dislodged a stream of sand that covers his boot and further aggravates his temper. "This is the worst stretch of country for military purposes that I've ever seen."

The general concentrates on the immediate tactical situation. "As long as that gun is there on the island, we can't occupy the trenches to the west of the fort. The gun position enfilades them perfectly. So we're stuck where we are trying to reduce them by the fire of two small howitzers. Eventually, that will work, but meanwhile, the men are suffering the cold and the wind. We can't get supplies or ammunition to them except at night, and there's no place to cook or even marshal the troops for an attack."

Inside the fort, Vernon and Ireland sit with their backs against the western earthworks and watch the preparations for the nighttime evacuation. There is a huge rushing sound as an artillery shell passes over on a low trajectory and buries itself in the sand atop the roof of the bombproof dugout. The resulting explosion throws shrapnel upward harmlessly with the low-angle energy absorbed by the sand. Ireland comments, "The name 'bombproof' is an accurate one. I would not believe it if I had not seen it repeatedly today. They are doing relatively little damage to us. We have no casualties so far, not even wounded. By the way, Vernon, instruct the men not to fire on parties carrying wounded Yankees back from the trenches." Vernon reflects on Ireland's mercy before he heard the follow-on comment. "Their problem is the supply line all the way back to New Orleans. A dead man makes no demands on the supply chain, but a wounded man makes severe demands. Their wounded serve us well."

The crack of a musket ended this comment. Shea's marksmen on the south earthworks were doing an excellent job of keeping the Union troops huddled down in the trenches. There was a small but steady flow of wounded back among the sandhills, but surprisingly no troops had been killed on either side.

* * *

The wind rises to a full norther in the afternoon. All hope is given up for a rapid water transport of the cavalry from Matagorda. The wind and low temperatures punish the infantry of both sides, but the Union artillery fires 155 shots and shell at the fort. Most of these pass over the fort and fall into Pass Cavallo. Ireland observes this and comments to Vernon, "The fort is well protected from bombardment."

"You can thank Otto for that. He insisted that the earthwork on the west and south sides be taller than the edge of the dugout so that no space exists for a shell to get into the dugout on a low trajectory. The high trajectories can pass over and hit the cannon facing the pass, but now there's no one out there."

* * *

On the night of the twenty-ninth, the evacuation of troops begins. Otto returns to the fort from the forward position of his howitzers and prepares to spike the main guns himself. The "spike" is a tapered steel rod with tiny ridges, much like a rattail file. It is sized to fit the touchhole of the gun. With a supply of spikes and a steel mallet, Otto walks along the battery of his carefully tended guns and makes them useless by driving the spike in place to achieve a "cold weld" to the gun's breech. Then with a swift sideways blow of the mallet, he breaks the brittle spike flush with the surface of the gun. This act prevents the insertion of any firing lock. The gun is disabled until a skilled machinist can drill out the hard tempered steel spike and restore the touchhole. Otto's emotions are mixed. Destroying the effectiveness of weapons he has carefully tended is a source of sadness. Doing an effective job of denying their use to the enemy is a matter of duty and pride.

* * *

In full ferry loads, the troops are taken to the main shore, formed up and started on the road to Indianola. Vernon personally carries the torch that starts the kindling in the forts supply rooms. When this is well under way and his own troops loaded on the ferry, he starts the kindling piles that lead to the fort's powder magazines. Vernon's men fire the bridges as they retreat and finally try to fire the ferry itself. Otto's howitzers fire over the bayous into the outer trenches, where the Union infantrymen huddle to escape the punishment of the cold, wet northern wind. Finally, he orders both guns to move out northward when he sees the Yankees capture the crew of the twenty-four-pounder on Bayoucos Island. *Damn,* he thinks, *they did not have time to spike that gun.* Fearing that the Union troops will turn the gun on the fleeing Confederates, he orders his guns out of sight into the darkness. He and his troops had long escaped before Union artillery men arrived at the lost gun and struggled to turn it around.

* * *

The Union infantry, noting the absence of musket fire and the beginning flames from the supply rooms, thinks of the warmth inside the fort and considers moving in. This dream stops when the first of the four powder magazines explodes. The troops simply wait until the explosions cease and enter to find the fort destroyed, but at least get shelter from the cold wet wind. Unfortunately, there is room for only one in five of the Union men in the fort's protection.

General Napoleon P. T. Banks congratulates himself on the achievement of his first objective, the capture of the fort, and the opening of Pass Cavallo. His troops are terribly punished by the full force of the norther and the lack of supplies, which cannot be unloaded from his ships in the storm-force winds.

PART V

Chapter Fifteen

December 1863-February 1864

The wind blows from the north for three days, straight into the faces of the men of Shea's battalion heading for Lavaca. Early in the morning of the first day, they pass to the west of Indianola. A few people line the roadside to speak to husbands, brothers, or sweethearts as they pass on their slow march northward. Some move back and forth along the line, searching for their loved one's face. Others, having found it, move slowly with the column that trudges steadily on toward Lavaca. Otto stands in the stirrups to scan the anxious faces, speaking or nodding to one or another, sometimes with the comment, "He's all right, ma'am. He's just back there a little ways." His eyes focus ahead, and the wind forms tears, which he wipes away with his sleeve. Then he spots a tall man in a Confederate army overcoat and, beside him, a small woman wrapped in a blanket that loops over her head and is held tightly in place by chilled red hands. It looks like Reuss, and the woman beside him must be Mary. He spurs the mule forward and, getting down, hobbles to her and enfolds her in his arms. After six hours in the saddle facing the cold wind, his knees cannot be trusted to hold him steady. She is shivering violently. He tries to sooth her, moving the blanket back to see her face, stained with tears but lovely still. "Your father is just fine, Mary. He's not injured, and he's holding up better than a lot of younger men."

Mary's shaking subsides for a moment as she cries. "I'm so worried about you. We've heard the firing of cannon all of yesterday, and there was no news. I'm so glad you are all right." One of his knees slips. "Are you all right?"

"I'm fine, Mary, just stiff and cold." Then over her head to Reuss, "We have had no casualties, but seven of Vernon's men were captured by the Yankees." Then back to Mary, "Die kinder?"

"They're at home with Frances. She's expecting, and I made her stay indoors so as not to harm the baby in this cold. They're just fine, Otto. Oh, it's been so long."

Otto holds Mary closer and feels the small body press to him through the blanket. "Liebschen, liebschen! I would love to just go home now. It's cruel to be so near and yet so far. I can't stay. We are on our way to Lavaca on this terrible coast road. The faster we get there, the safer we will be. It would be a slaughter if the Union ships came through the pass and caught us in the open on this road." Mary's head burrowed into his shoulder.

"Reuss, will you take Mary home, see that there's a big fire in the cookstove, and sit her down in front of it?"

"I'll do better than that, Otto. I'll heat up a couple of bricks and wrap them in dish towels to put under her feet. Don't worry about Mary or the kids."

Otto gives Mary a last hug and tenderly wraps the blanket around her face. "Kiss Lina for me."

He swings up onto the mule and walks it briskly ahead. The wind brings tears to his eyes. He is unsure whether it's the wind or his sorrow for the state of his family and the loss of the fort.

* * *

On December 2, the battalion reaches their old encampment on Agua Dulce Creek. The canvas catchments for the cisterns, taken from the fort to deny the Union a source of water, are again set up as lean-tos. They give protection from the wind and a place for cooking fires and for those who are ill. The men recover in this familiar campground, thinking of Christmas 1862 when they were well, comfortable, and flushed with victory over the Union ships. What a contrast. There would be no cooking contest this year. For the moment, it is enough to be sheltered.

* * *

General Magruder envisions that he is now caught between two Union forces invading Texas. First, the one at Fort Esperanza, which now also holds Saluria and its dock facilities. Second is the army on the Red River. He concentrates forces between these two. While assuring the governor and the people of west Texas that he will not abandon them, he removes virtually all military forces from the west. The result is an increase in Indian raids and the inevitable horror and cruelty that accompanies them. In 1863, Indian raiders kill twenty civilians and burn fifteen homes. Soldiers from western Texas, finding themselves on the Texas coast unable to protect their families, are individually deserting and, in some cases, nearing mutiny of entire units.

* * *

"Well, that settles the hash!" Major Ireland says as he reads the dispatch handed to him in the mess hall. "Gentlemen, you have wondered what is in store for us. Now we know. We are to take the road from Texana to Columbia to the east bank of the Brazos River. There we are to go downstream ten miles and set up camp."

Vernon, tugging on his mustache, offers, "That is a nice place. I'm ready for a change of scenery. The Brazos River has some good camping grounds for the men. At that site, we can move to counter an invasion up the Brazos or over to the Colorado River further east. If no river invasions are undertaken by the Union, we can march into Galveston to protect that port."

"That's exactly how I see it too," says Ireland. "I'm going to broadly interpret my orders by delaying a day until the wind subsides. We'll camp the first night at Texana." At that site, he sees a familiar face leading troops back the way he has come from Lavaca. He calls out, "Get down and set a spell. You can even have a cup of corn coffee."

This is seen as humorous by the captain leading the troops. Turning to his first lieutenant, he says, "Camp on the other side of the Lavaca River. I'm going to visit here and get some information. I'll see you in about an hour." Getting down off his horse, he says, "Ireland, you have gotten majors leave since I last saw you. Congratulations!"

They talk for a while, exchanging information on camping spots in each direction and sharing cups of corn coffee heavily laced with sugar. It tastes bad, but it is black and sweet and, after two and a half years of war, is approaching acceptability. Ireland explains that he was ordered to the Brazos River and asks how it was that the other unit is tracing exactly the reverse path. The captain unfolds his orders and points silently to the middle of the page. Ireland reads:

> *Destroy the wharves, railroad, burning the ties, burning and destroying the engines, flats, coaches, etc. from Lavaca to Victoria, and also the storehouses and every house excepting such as are actually occupied by the people at Indianola, Powderhorn, and Lavaca, giving the people one day's notice to leave if possible. A complete destruction of all these things will be made.*
>
> *By order, General John B. Magruder*

Ireland whistles, takes a swig of the hot fluid, turns his head away, and says, "Damn! I see it now. If you're gonna destroy the place, you use troops from somewhere else, not the hometown boys." The captain simply nods, saying, "I'm gonna join my troops now. I wish you luck on the Brazos."

Ireland's thoughts are in conflict. He can see the military need to limit the Yankees' ability to move by railroad, but he also sees the hopes and dreams of the people in these communities being destroyed. What will they do after the war when they were expecting to become the transportation center of Texas to the West? No wonder Magruder is sending the local boys away and bringing in outsiders to do the destruction. He pours out the coffee. It's too bitter to swallow.

* * *

Three days later, the battalion is being ferried to the east side of the Brazos River. The assistant surgeon sits his mule alongside Ireland, watching in silence as the units load. He says, "Major, there's an old cavalry saying that the coffee tastes better if it's brewed upstream of the horses. We don't have either horses or coffee, but I'm sure you have thought that our health would be better the further we are upstream in this big encampment. I expect Magruder is gonna pile a lot of folks in here before we're through."

"Yup, I thought that we might just slow down a little and see who is coming behind us. If there's nobody back there, we can go down this east bank until we see the next unit. If there is someone behind us, we'll let 'em pass through while we do some fishin' to stretch out our supplies. Let's go dip a line in that river. I think I heard a cavalry kind of sound upstream just now."

In five minutes, a cavalry captain is given permission to pass through the battalion. The next day, Ireland moves down the stream and finds a good campground, where a clean-looking creek runs into the Brazos. There is plenty of wood and grass. The mules are picketed downstream of the creek, and Lieutenant French is sent in search of the local headquarters to report that Ireland's battalion of Hobby's Eighth Texas Infantry is in camp.

French returns with an order requiring two infantry platoons to move back to the Columbia-Texana Road and march west. They are to search for a group of sixty deserters, infantrymen who have taken their arms and are going west to protect their families on the frontier from the Comanche raids. Ireland assembles the two platoon leaders and a first lieutenant from the infantry companies and gives them their instructions. "My orders require you to search for these men as far as Texana. I am ordered to return them 'with hands tied' to General Magruder. If they resist arrest, I am ordered to fire upon them." He pauses and looks at each of the three men in turn. Then he continues, "Those are my orders—if I catch them. There might be any number of reasons why I can't catch them. They might be ahead of me. They might be hiding in the woods. They might have broken up and are traveling in small groups. Your men might have been talking in ranks, and they heard you coming. They might be on another road." With his head lowered, he says. "If you are unable to find them, it would not be a black mark against you. Men going to protect their families can be very clever." Looking up, he asks, "Are there any questions?" There were none. In parting, he says, "When you get to Lavaca, wait three days and then return." Everyone nods.

When the two platoons are assembled on the road and starting their march, the first lieutenant, turning to look at his companion, says, "Well, we have the orders that Magruder issued, and we have a lot of reasons why they might not be carried out. Where do they teach lawyers like him about words?"

His companion offers, "My daddy always said lawyers learn from the criminals they associate with."

"Your daddy is a very bright man."

* * *

By early January, it is evident that the Union commander of the invasion is completely hampered by a lack of transportation. There is no large supply of water within twenty miles of the coast. This is discovered when his twenty thousand troops arrive on Matagorda Island finding water supplies that will support only five hundred men. A complete division of three thousand troops occupies Indianola to establish a position on Matagorda Bay. Fort Esperanza is held by three hundred colored troops and Saluria by two hundred white troops. The invasion of Texas from the coast is put on hold, and fifteen thousand Yankees are shipped back to Louisiana to storm Texas from the Red River. The troops in Indianola are quartered in the houses of the citizens. The division commander gives orders that the citizens be treated with respect. He hopes that this may persuade some to throw in their lot with the Union.

* * *

Erdmuthe hears the knock at the front door and dusts flour from her hands on her apron. She walks to the door, wondering who this could be in the middle of the morning. Opening the door, she sees three Union officers dressed in dark-blue uniforms that are clean but rumpled. Addressing the one with captain's bars, she says, "Why are you here?"

The young man, hat in hand, replies, "We are to be quartered in civilian houses, Mrs. Thompson, and we are calling on you to make arrangements."

"Which of you is the senior officer of this group?"

"I am, ma'am, I'm the captain."

Mutti turns to the captain and smiles, looking directly into his eyes. "I am Mrs. Thompson, and I'm the senior officer of this house. Please come in and be seated at the table." She takes her place at the head of the table, and the captain sits at the foot, his lieutenants on each side. "Gentlemen, I am sure that you would prefer to be at home with your families rather than here in Texas. Please be assured that I share that preference with you. However, we must accept what fate has given us and put the best face on it."

The captain replies, "We wish to discuss the arrangements."

"Of course. The arrangements will be as follows. If you have any complaints, these will be made through your senior officer to me. Similarly, if I have any complaints, I will convey them to your senior officer." This was answered with nods around the table. Mutti continued, "You will furnish your own linen and arrange for its washing. You will arrange for the cleaning of your rooms. There is one with two beds and one with a large single." All of this is said to the captain with a direct gaze into his eyes and a warm smile on her face. "You will arrange for your own meals, or if you prefer, you may bring your rations to me, and I will prepare and serve them for a reasonable fee. If you choose that route, then bring me some flour, and I'll be pleased to make a pecan *kuchen* for you. There is no coffee, so if you wish some with your meals, please bring beans to me, and I will grind them and brew the coffee for you, again for a reasonable fee. You will not entertain ladies in your quarters or bring them into the house. Should you desire to have a supper prepared for your senior officers, that can be arranged. I will plan the menu, and you will bring the supplies. Do you have any questions?"

"No, ma'am."

"Then I will show you the way out." Standing at the door, she smilingly says, "I do hope that you have an enjoyable day."

As they walked back to headquarters, the captain, raised in a fine Boston family, turns to one of the lieutenants, saying, "Why is it that when she is talking to me, I feel in the presence of a grand and lovely lady, but when I talk to her, it's like addressing a senior colonel?"

"I'm sure I don't know, sir, but I do know what a German *kuchen* is. Do you think we could find some flour?"

In the headquarters, a colonel stops the young captain to ask, "Does your quartering go well?"

"Yes, sir."

"Does the civilian understand the arrangements?"

"I don't think there is any doubt of that, sir."

"Good, carry on, Captain."

The captain does, wondering where he could locate some flour.

Chapter Sixteen

January 1864

At the Brazos camp, time drags with the men chiefly occupied in keeping warm. Supplies of cornmeal and beans drawn from the depot at Columbia are adequate but monotonous. The supply of catfish in the river is depleted as the men wait for a move by the Yankees. The two platoons of infantry return from their unsuccessful search for the deserters.

In their tent, Beyer and Otto smoke their pipes, the filling reduced to crumbled bark of wild grapevines. It gave off white smoke, but that is the only similarity to the unobtainable tobacco. Beyer asks, "Why does Magruder have us here on the east bank of the Brazos River?"

"It's a peculiarity of Texas. The rivers run from northwest to southeast, the way the land slopes. The roads run east and west, and they are thirty miles from the coast at the closest. If you are going to invade Texas and get to the cotton and particularly the cattle, you have to come up some river to get to a road and then move east or west. Magruder figures he must defend those rivers to keep the Yankees from getting to the roads. I think he's got us here so that we can defend Brazos River, or move over to the Colorado."

"What about the Yankees moving up Matagorda Bay?"

"That's a problem, but fresh water is scarce there. The road to San Antonio from Texana doesn't promise much water for a force of twenty thousand."

"So we sit here until the Yankees decide just where they are going to get thirsty."

"Once again, Beyer, you put your finger on the nut of it."

* * *

In January, scouts report the departure of the main force from Saluria; and soon after, orders come for the battalion to move to Galveston. Ireland finds this puzzling as his command is being split. Company A and the infantry are ordered to Virginia Point, while Company B is to go to a place called Redoubt #3. He concludes that he will stay with Vernon and the infantry and let Otto take care of himself.

The men are marginally happier on the road than in the camp. The scenery is changing. Although there is more exposure to the cold and the wind, the exercise beats sitting around in tents looking at the same faces day after day.

Three days after leaving the Brazos, Ireland stops his horse at the end of a causeway leading to Galveston Island and addresses the sentry at the gate of Fort Green, "We are ordered to Virginia Point and Redoubt #3. How do we get there?"

"Sir, that road back there 'bout a hundred yards leads east to Virginia Point. You can just barely see it stickin' out into the bay 'bout five miles." He gestures to make his point then continues, "Redoubt #3 is on the island. You go across this causeway then left through Galveston City all the way out the other end. Then about halfway to Fort Point, you can just see it, that's Fort Bankhead. Redoubt #3 is in there." This is also accompanied with gestures. It is clear to Ireland that his men will be looking at each other across Galveston Bay. They'll be separated by three miles of water or ten miles of road. He returns the sentry's salute and, turning to Otto, says, "Take the two twelve-pounders with you and their teams. Also take two of the wagons and report in to the fort commander when you arrive. You heard the directions?"

"Yes, sir." Turning in the saddle, Otto says to Beyer and Sergeant Noll, "John, have the men follow me onto the causeway. Put one gun and the wagons in the middle of the company, the other gun at the rear. Beyer, I want you to bring up the rear. I want no stragglers and no broken wagons." With that, he turns his mule toward the causeway but stops just before the entrance ramp. *What is that in the water?* Looking closer, he can hardly believe what he sees. Next to the shore, where the water is quiet, there is ice at least an inch and a half thick. Looking out, he can see that the ice extends several hundred feet from shore. The saltwater bay is frozen! Surely this has not happened before, at least not in recent memory. When he is on the causeway, he can see snow on the boards, at least an inch deep. There are comments that this is the coldest winter on record, but the sight turns his thoughts to care of the men under these circumstances. All the way through Galveston, this concern is uppermost in his mind.

At the gate to Fort Bankhead, he asks the sentry to report his company in to the fort commander and request instructions. While waiting, he surveys the fort. It is obviously new, made after Magruder captured Galveston a year ago. He heard that one hundred slaves were used in its construction, and now the height of the earthworks confirms this. It must have taken them three or four months, he calculates.

The strangest thing is a railway entering the fort through the gate where he stands. Looking along the tracks, he sees not an engine but a cannon mounted on a cart and pointing out through an embrasure at the harbor. What a strange place. He will have a host of questions for his fellow officers here.

"Captain Schnaubert?" a voice calls from the gateway. Looking over, he sees a young captain and confirms with a salute that this is Company B of Hobby's Eighth Texas Infantry, and he is its commander.

"Welcome to Fort Bankhead. Follow me, and I'll show you where your company will be located."

Otto follows the captain, walking through the mud. A few sprigs of rye grass show that some effort was made to cover the massive earthworks and prevent them washing away in the spring rains. His company area is at the east end of the fort. Mounds of trash show that it was used recently, and the occupants made no effort to clean it up. Otto asks directions to the office of the fort commander, thanks the captain, and turns to Beyer and John Noll. Seeing anguish on their faces at the condition of the fort, he says, "Let's put this place right. Clean it up. Place the tents against the eastern breastwork. Erect a lean-to at the north end of the tent line, open to the south. We can use it as a mess hall and company headquarters. The men can warm themselves at the cooking fires. See if there's someplace outside the fort with grass for the mules. I'm going to pay my—umm—respects to the fort commander."

* * *

The forts commander sits in a tiny wooden building that backs on the north breastwork. It gives protection from the winter wind but a terrible exposure to the sun in summer. Otto salutes, saying, "Otto L. Schnaubert, Commander B Company, Eighth Texas Infantry reporting in."

Returning his salute, the major says, "I'm glad to have you here. Your men looked good as they entered the fort. Do you have any questions?" Otto is full of questions but limited himself to those necessary for short-time guidance. "We have six officers and ninety-six men. What are the messing arrangements?"

"I don't maintain a mess but visit the officers' mess of each company in the fort. You'll have to make your own arrangements. Commissary supplies are distributed by wagon from Fort Green each Monday. Have your man meet the wagon at the west gate about 2:00 p.m. I take it you have brought your own ordnance supplies for the two cannons you have?"

"Yes, sir. We have two hundred rounds for each gun, shot, shell, and canister. Shall we emplace the guns?"

"Yes, come outside with me, and I'll show you where they should go." Otto follows, with the major leading the way outside and up onto the top of the north breastwork. Pointing back into the fort, he says, "I want your twelve-pounders in the northeast corner, one pointing north into the harbor and one pointing west to cover the breastwork. You can see that the embrasures are already cut."

Otto points a little west of north, asking, "Is that Virginia Point, just beyond the island?"

"Yes, it is. I believe the rest of your battalion is there. That's Pelican Island. It forms the north side of the channel into Galveston Harbor. As you can see, the channel is rather narrow, and the guns of Fort Point cover it at the inlet. We will not have ships in range of our guns until they have gotten past Fort Point."

"When is the senior officers' meeting, sir?"

"We don't have regular meetings. They are called when they are necessary." With that, the major leaps down from the breastwork and walks to his building. He turns, saying, "Unless you have any questions, Captain, let me say again—welcome to our fort."

Otto, thinking that it is probably best not to have questions, says, "Thank you, sir." Turning, he walks back to his company location. Seeing George, he says, "Make room in the lean-to for an officers' mess, which I'll also use as an office."

Otto surveys the inside of the fort, finding two other companies in place with tents against the west and south breastworks. He walks along the north breastwork to examine a large sixty-four-pounder siege gun that is emplaced about halfway to his tent line. It looks to be in superior condition, mounted on a railway cart with its muzzle poking out in the direction of the entrance channel. Walking over, he finds the gun to be too clean and free of pits to have been in service long. It is dark and looks polished. He lays his hand on the breech and finds, to his surprise, not cold iron, but wood! He walks around and finds it to be a perfect replica, but made of wood, obviously turned on a lathe, sanded, and painted to resemble cast iron. Whoever has done the work certainly knows cannons. Even the turnbulls that sit on the carriage are the right length and diameter. He determines to solve this puzzle and, turning, walks to the tents on the south breastwork.

As he walks, a sergeant approaches, salutes, and says, "Good afternoon, Captain."

"I have just arrived with my company over there, and I'd like to meet your commander."

"That is easily arranged, sir. Follow me." They walk to a large tent in the center of the line where the sergeant, saluting a man inside the tent, says, "Captain, there is an officer here who wishes to speak with you." The man walks out of the tent with a question on his face.

"I'm Otto Schnaubert. That's my Company B of the Eighth Texas Infantry that just arrived today. I've called on the fort commander and thought I'd introduce myself to you."

The captain introduces himself, saying, "He would not make the effort to introduce us, would he? Please come in and have a cup of real coffee?"

"I haven't had real coffee in three years. I don't know if I can stand that, but I'd sure like to find out."

The man pours a cup, and Otto inhales a fragrance nearly forgotten. After a sip, he says, "That's wonderful. How did you manage to come by this?"

"The blockade runners arrive in port about every other day. I simply meet the ship's captain and explain how we protect him by keeping the Yankee ships at bay. Give him a few pointers on tide and best time to depart. He'd have to be downright mean not to make me a present." Otto has his first real laugh in a month.

"The merchants in Galveston don't have merchandise in their stores until a blockade runner comes in. Then they open until it's all sold and stay closed till the next one arrives."

"I saw something today that puzzles me. Maybe you could tell me about that wooden sixty-four-pounder on the railroad cart?"

"Oh, the Quaker Gun, that's Magruder's idea. There is a foundry here in Galveston that makes cannons. It is staffed with a bunch of Germans, and they do great work but don't speak a word of English. Anyway, Prince John did not have enough guns to fill all the embrasures of the forts he built after he captured the city. He gets this idea that if he has a railway that runs around through all the forts, then he can shift guns wherever he wanted them. That is a pretty good idea, but he tops that by telling the Germans to make him some fake cannons out of wood. They're not about to do shoddy work, so they go over to the mainland and cut themselves a bunch of Sycamore logs. They bring 'em back and put 'em on the lathes just like they were iron, which they had run out of. They turn 'em down exactly to spec, then sand and paint 'em. That's how Prince John gets his forts filled up." Otto enjoys his second laugh of the day.

"What a story. I would not believe it if I had not seen that one there. If it fooled me at fifty feet, it must have fooled the Yankees at three miles."

"You haven't heard the best part of the story. Initially, it did fool 'em. They get out their telescopes and watch carefully as the guns move from one fort to another. Then the whole thing falls through. I was at Fort Point then. The Yankees signal a flag of truce and come ashore in a small boat for some reason. The fort commander tells them he doesn't want 'em to get too close and spy on his fort. They might decide to invade it. The Yankee, real cool like, says he was watching through the telescope one day when two men picked up a six-thousand-pound gun to put it on a carriage. There is complete silence. Then he says, 'We would never invade a fort that had such strong men.'" Otto doubles over in laughter.

They talked on for a while, with Otto inviting the captain over to visit but warning he could not equal the coffee. On his way back to the lean-to, he laughs again and realizes he has not felt this good in a year.

* * *

During the next month, Otto goes into Galveston to get a picture of the place. What he finds saddens him. Crime is rife within the city, and the citizens blame it on the Confederate troops. There is some truth in this view. The army rations are of terrible quality. This prompts the less-disciplined troops to steal chickens and pigs from the citizens. In one case, a citizen shoots a soldier who is stealing his pig. The soldier dies, and his unit comes into town, captures the man, and stabs him to death. The army command thinks that military rule is the answer. This simply enflames the citizens more and does nothing to reduce crime. The army and the populace are at an impasse.

* * *

In February, Otto's company is ordered to Virginia Point, and Vernon's company comes to Redoubt #3. He assembles his officers and NCOs, saying, "We are going to Virginia Point. You remember from our trip in, that will take us the entire length of Galveston City. When we make that trip, I want this company to be an example of what a Confederate army unit can be. I want the mules brushed, the harness oiled, the caissons clean, and your uniforms as clean as they can be. Most of the musicians of the battalion band are in this company. They will form up at the rear of the company with their instruments. We will march in step, and the band will play 'Yellow Rose of Texas' all the way through Galveston. We will show them what it means to be from Indianola." They did.

When the company passes the business section of Galveston, the men are ordered to sing. They do.

There's a yellow rose of Texas, that I am going to see
Nobody else could miss her, not half as much as me
She cried so when I left her, it like to broke my heart
And if I ever find her, we nevermore will part

She's the sweetest little rosebud that Texas ever knew,
Her eyes are bright as diamonds, they sparkle like the dew;
You may talk about your Clementine, and sing of Rosalee
But the yellow rose of Texas is the only girl for me

As the company passes, citizens hear the music and rush to the street to see what is under way. There are few cheers, but nearly everyone feels better about Galveston and its sad plight after they pass.

CHAPTER SEVENTEEN

February 1864

At Virginia Point, the arrival of Company B at the West Gate is expected. A first lieutenant meets Otto and escorts him to the location just vacated by Vernon's company. The area is spotless, but worn grass shows where tents and a lean-to have been. Otto tells Beyer that a duplication of Vernon's arrangements will be fine. A lieutenant escorts him to the fort commander's office. The major looks up, rises, and walks to Otto, who salutes, saying, "Otto Schnaubert, commanding Company B, Eighth Texas Infantry, reporting my company in the fort."

The major smiles warmly and introduces himself, "The reputation of your unit precedes you, sir. Captain Vernon tells me of your actions at Indianola, Lavaca, and Fort Esperanza. I'm pleased to have you here. Sit down for a moment, let's talk." Indicating a chair for Otto, the major sits in front of his desk and continues, "We have a different situation here than in Galveston. It's true that our commissary stores are equally bad. They come from the same place. But we do not have a large civilian population nearby. Hence, crime has not been a problem as it has been there. We have extensive stores on site if you need to replenish anything for your company. I'm sure you have many questions. I'll stop and let you ask them."

Otto, struck by the contrast to the commander at Redoubt #3, warms greatly to the major. He asks, "What are the messing provisions for the men?"

"Each company maintains its own mess for enlisted men. I have a single mess here for all officers. It's large, just over twenty, but we strive to keep order." The last is said with a smile. "Also, I hold a meeting with the senior officers here in my office on Tuesdays,

Thursdays, and Saturdays, at 9:00 a.m. Additional meetings are called when necessary in emergencies. Fortunately, there are not many. The Yankees stay on the other side of the bar, which is well beyond the range of our guns. Even in the channel, they would be beyond the range of twelve-pounders. So I will ask you to emplace your guns on the north breastwork covering the land approach to the fort. You will find two embrasures there. It's close to your tent location."

They talked on briefly, and then the major, rising, says, "Welcome to the fort." Otto smiles and, turning, walks out of headquarters back to the company area.

* * *

The next day, Otto goes to the depot where supplies are stored. He requisitions two pairs of shoes, two blankets, and six iron pots. The shoes and blankets, for his own use, are charged against his pay. The pots are for the lean-to. Those used for cooking are nearly worn out and are replaced by these new ones. Back at the company area, he explains the idea to John Noll. In the depot, he saw a large pile of soft coal. Sometime in the past, it was ordered for a steamboat that no longer docked at the fort. The old cooking pots will make good coal stoves for cooking and also for warming the men coming off watch. It is still the coldest winter on record. Both Otto and John Noll, with German upbringing, have used coal stoves. But the younger Texas men have never seen such contraptions. Noll takes a wagon over to the depot and requisitions a substantial load of coal. A few holes are drilled in the bottom of the old pots to feed air. Kindling is laid with coal on top. With the kindling lit, in ten minutes, the coal is glowing. One of the old pots is arranged for cooking with a pot of stew on top. Another is devoted to warming men that are on watch. The stew is the only healthy way to prepare the beef, which is well on its way to being unusable. The Texas lads are amazed at these rocks that burn.

* * *

The men consistently complain, since arriving at Virginia Point, that mosquitoes eat them alive on watch, particularly at night. Otto requisitions canvas and mosquito screen that convert the lean-to into a protected area for the men off watch. Nothing can be done about the men on watch, except to insist on gloves and long sleeves buttoned tightly at the wrist.

The Indianola fisherman in the company find a skiff pulled up ashore behind the point. Naturally, they use it, with a tree limb as a pole, to explore the water around the point. To their surprise, at one location, they pull up a small dead tree covered with oysters. Frying them, they produce a delicious treat. Arranging two wooden poles to form an oyster rake, they begin to pull up dead trees in quantity. They always leave a couple oysters on each tree and lower it back to grow more oysters. The fried oysters go a long way in supplementing the taste of the rotten beef.

* * *

Shortly after coming to Virginia Point, Otto awakens to find he is ill. He declines dinner that night and, in a fit of nausea, vomits a black bile. He has lived long enough in Texas to know this as a symptom of what the Latinos call "vomito negro," which the English call yellow fever. He turns the company over to Beyer, who notifies the fort commander. Otto is confined to quarters. His tent becomes a quarantine area.

The year 1964 proved to be Galveston's worst year of the decade for yellow fever. Conditions on the island are so bad that one hotel is closed down and converted to a hospital for recovering soldiers. Otto is confined to quarters for six weeks. His health does not improve, and he is given a sick leave to be spent at home.

CHAPTER EIGHTEEN

April 1864

Mary washes the breakfast dishes as the knock sounds on the front door. "Frances, can you answer that? My hands are wet."

"Mary, it's for you."

Drying her hands on the apron, Mary walks to the door and sees a young soldier, tall, very lean, his mismatched pants and shirt covered with a thick layer of dust. His cap is held under his left elbow, and the right hand extends a letter in her direction. "Mrs. Schnaubert, your husband wanted me to deliver this letter to you. I just brought it in with the dispatches from Galveston. I'm sorry to be so dirty, but it's a hard three-day ride."

Thanking him, Mary sees that the letter is addressed in Otto's handwriting and moves to the kitchen to fetch a knife to open it. Holding her breath, she slits the envelope; $500 in Confederate funds fall out. Surprised and puzzled at this small fortune, she hurries to read the letter. It explains that now he is in the Confederate States Army and has back pay for four months of $520. He is keeping twenty dollars for his own expenses and sends $500 to her for safekeeping. If possible she should convert it to U.S. dollars. He now fears for the future of Confederate currency after the defeat at Gettysburg and the fall of Vicksburg, which cuts the South in half.

"Frances, would you mind the baby so that I can go over to your mother's house? Otto's all right, but he's asked me to do something I don't understand, and I value Mutti's advice."

When she arrives, Mary is breathless and realizes that she has been running all the way. The door opens, and she is offered a cup of tea and a chance to settle down in the kitchen. Mutti smiles and asks, "Now just what is it that sends you here in such a swivet?" Mary explains about the letter and the $500, adding that she has no idea what to do about it. This was greeted with "Oh, is that all?" and the statement, "We'll take care of that tomorrow. Could you come by at ten o'clock?" Mary leaves no more knowledgeable when than she arrived but feeling much better about the whole thing.

* * *

The next day, Mutti and Mary start for town. After a few steps, she says, "Mary, please carry this plate for me. My bones are getting old, and I may need them in good shape before the morning is out." Mary finds that puzzling. She does not always understand Frances's mother, but she does have confidence in her. And so, they walk to town and through the front door of Henry Runge's bank. Inside, Mutti says, "Mary, I will take that now." She holds the plate in front of her as they walk through the bank to Henry's office in the rear. His door is guarded by a tall lady of perhaps thirty, whose tightly corseted form reveals ample bosom and well-rounded hips, confirming that Henry Runge is not immune to female beauty. Anyone acquainted with his wife, Julia, eighteen years his junior, knows that already. Mutti smiles and announces, "We have a gift for Mr. Runge."

The lady seems to recognize her and announces through the door, "Mrs. Thompson is here with a gift for you." And then with a tiny smile, "Please enter."

With Mutti in the lead, they walk into Runge's office as he rises to greet them.

"Henry, I remember seeing you at Frances's wedding and thinking to myself, I must do something nice for him. I know how wonderful Julia's apple fritters are, and I could never compete with them, but maybe a *kuchen* with pecans would be welcome. It'll keep well here in your office, and you could have a slice from time to time."

This last is said as the cover is removed from the plate with a flourish. The odor of warm coffee cake fills the office. Henry's face beams with delight. He knows that Mutti will have a hook somewhere in the bait, but this is delightful bait indeed. The cake takes him back to his mother's kitchen in Bremen. Momentarily, he is a boy again.

Mutti introduces Mary as Captain Schnaubert's wife, which Runge acknowledges.

"I remember Otto. He did surveying for the railroad track before the war. And he built the mule railway at the fort. How is he?" Mary replies favorably on his health. Erdmuthe picks up the initiative by slicing a piece of the cake for Henry and turns the conversation to early days in Indianola. Mary watches and marvels. When Mutti speaks to a man, there just is no one else present but the two of them. Her eyes never leave his, and that engaging smile seems to warm the room like a well-stoked woodstove.

Henry wonders where he had been when this charming woman was a young widow thirteen years ago. He makes a mental note to buy Julia a present for their thirteenth wedding anniversary and immediately knows the answer to that idle question. Anyway, that sneaky Alsatian Charles Dickerson snatched her up before her widowhood was a year old.

Finally, Mutti says that Mary wishes to open an account at the bank. Henry knows that this cannot be the hook, saying, "That would be wonderful, Mrs. Schnaubert." He waits for the hook to emerge. It is not long in coming. The funds are in Confederate dollars and the account should be in U.S. dollars. Well, if that is the only hook, then it is doable.

He says, "There are problems with that, mainly the source of U.S. dollars. We do occasionally see some from trades in Mexico. In that, we are fortunate, inland cities haven't seen U.S. dollars in three years. We could exchange your funds at thirteen cents on the dollar."

Erdmuthe frowns slightly, and the room's temperature drops several degrees. She says, "Henry, I thought the exchange was closer to fifteen cents."

Henry, blushing, slightly replies, "Let me check, we don't often get a request for exchange." He disappears into the bank briefly and returns, smiling, "Yes, I think we could make that exchange at fifteen cents."

Mutti smiles and offers another slice of cake.

Mary leaves the bank with a deposit slip for seventy-five U.S. dollars and a boundless admiration for Mutti, who simply assures her, "All that men ever want is just to be treated nicely."

* * *

Mary arrives at her house to find the young soldier who delivered the letter waiting on the front porch. Mary greets him, and he, with his cap in hand, says, "Mrs. Schnaubert, I'm not supposed to tell you this, but I think it would be best if you heard the straight story and not some rumor. Captain Schnaubert came down with yellow fever about a month ago. You can't imagine what an unhealthy place that Galveston is. Anyway, he's through the worst, and he's not gonna die of it. That was what I wanted to tell you. Also, I want to say he's a fine man that takes good care of his troops, and I'm proud to serve under him. Now, ma'am, I gotta git back."

Turning from the porch, he mounts his horse and is off. Dust flies up from the road, and Mary thinks of a dozen things she wants to ask and say to Otto. The news on Otto's health is a blow coming after the pleasant day with Mutti. Her shoulders slump, and she suddenly feels very weary. She enters the house to see how Lina Katlyn is fairing. Tears form in her eyes. She starts to prepare supper for herself, Frances, and Lina. Frances, sensing the problem, embraces Mary, saying, "What is it?"

"Otto's sick and he needs me and I can't go to him and Lina needs me and Charly needs me too." This was followed by a torrent of tears that frightened Lina, who grabbed her mother's skirt and holds on tightly. Charly watched from the crib, puzzled by the noise.

* * *

The young soldier's report is partly correct; Otto isn't dying of yellow fever, but he isn't getting well either. Finally, he determines to go home and recuperate there. Otto locates John Noll and asks if he will find the mule named Maggie and saddle her. John does and figures he could keep this in the family when Otto rides out the gate of the fort at Virginia Point. Actually, Otto has a two-month medical leave in his pocket. He might get caught by Yankees, but he is not going to be arrested by rebs.

After the terrible winter, the weather is warm in this April, and Otto has no problem sleeping outside. He follows in reverse the same path that brought him to Galveston six months ago. The wild flowers are in bloom in the fields, and he thinks that this Texas is sometimes very beautiful. Maggie enjoys the new rye grass and the fresh water in the creeks as a change from the dry forage and brackish water at Galveston. Also, there are nowhere near as many mosquitoes. A mule could get to like this country.

Ten days after he leaves Galveston Bay, Otto is in the woods at Lavaca, waiting for night to fall so that he can enter Indianola. He puzzles about the guard that the Union army will put on the road between Lavaca and Indianola. Most likely, this will be a squad of men in a shallow trench without field glasses and watching for cavalry on the Lavaca road. He decides that he will ride over toward Green Lake and enter the town from the west. That way, he will be behind the guard when he comes close enough to be noticed. If he is quiet, it just might work out. His decision to leave Galveston is the right one. The thoughts of home leave him feeling better but still terribly weak.

His ruse would have worked, but the Yankees withdrew from Indianola on April 15, a week before. When the moon is up, Otto has Maggie in the barn and raps gently on the back door. Mary cannot believe her eyes. *Otto is here!* She hugs him eagerly. It is evident that he has lost weight and has a sort of sour smell. She lights a candle and sees that his face is drawn even though he is smiling. She hugs him again. Her breath comes in quick gasps while her heart races. *Does he need food? Does he need rest? What comes first?*

Otto answers her question simply, "Mary, I'm very tired, but I'm home." She opts for rest first, helps him to the bed, and pulls off his boots. Otto's eyes close, and he breathes a long sigh. Mary pulls the blanket over him and sits for a time just watching. Frances, who sleeps on the couch in the parlor, comes to sit with her and wishes that her husband Will was safe at home.

Mary arranges for her brother to come and take Maggie. He saddles her and rides to the Noll farm. Maggie is happy to graduate from dry fodder to fresh rye grass, but the brackish water is a letdown.

Otto begins to gain weight under Mary's care, and his depressed thoughts subside. Perhaps the world is not as hopeless as it seemed in Galveston. At least the Yankees are gone from Indianola, and this time without sacking the place.

* * *

The knock on the back door startles Otto, lying in bed. He hears the back door open and a small gasp, then is surprised to see Will Moore holding Frances and kissing her neck. When Will and Frances are each reassured that the other is safe and well, Mary says, "Otto is here, recovering from yellow fever. He's not contagious, and I know he'd like to talk with you."

Will steps into the bedroom, "Otto, you have lost a lot of weight. I'm glad you're here where the ladies can care for you. How do you feel?"

"I feel like I have been run over by a wagon. But let's not talk about me. What are you up to? The last I heard you were on the *Carr* showing them how to use cannon on a cotton-clad ship."

"When Major Shea first started to build his navy on Matagorda Bay, things went very well. The *Carr* was filled with gun crews from experienced artillery companies. You recall that was when I volunteered. We were no match for Yankee deep-water ships, but we were a threat to their small gunboats. We did good service when they tried to send troops up Matagorda Peninsula. But then Shea wanted to equip other ships, and our crews were siphoned off to man them." Otto confirms this with a nod.

"Things on the *Carr* went downhill. That Bradfute fellow sent us a bunch of no-good deserters as crew replacements. Our captain sent a letter, saying they did not know their nostrils from a double-barrel shotgun. We got a laugh out of that, but it really was not funny. You could not trust your shipmates. So I volunteered to do some scouting. I locate myself over on DeCrows Point with a telescope and watch the Yankees in Saluria and at the fort. That's only about a mile, and you'd be surprised what you can see with a good telescope at that distance. Well, maybe you would not be surprised, but most folks would."

"All right, tell me what's going on with the Yankees."

"It's downright peculiar. The fort is staffed with about three hundred black troops and Saluria with two hundred whites. They have got a lot of new guns at the fort, but they had some kind of mutiny. At least there was a lot of shouting and fist shaking between the blacks and some white troops. They shot one of the blacks. But they have put a lot of work into the fort. I saw them carrying railroad rails off a sloop up to the fort and putting them into the bombproof. I think those were the rails left over after Magruder had the railroad torn up between Lavaca and Victoria."

"Isn't that a trifle dangerous, you sitting out there in front of the Yankees?"

"Naw. I get in a house that they destroyed when they were getting ready to march up the Matagorda Peninsula and move on the Brazos River. I sit behind some broken siding. They could be right on the peninsula and not see me. I have got a small sloop that I tie up in a cove back from the house and out of sight. When I need to report, I just sail at night over here to Indianola—'course sometimes I need to report up here to Frances." The last was accompanied with a pinch on her rump.

Otto reflects that Frances does look a little heavier than he remembers, probably the result of some earlier reporting. In the morning, Will is not in evidence, having left to sail back to DeCrows Point three hours before sunup.

Part VI

Chapter Nineteen

May 1864

"Are you Capt. Otto L. Schnaubert?" The voice is firm and carries a tone of command. Otto's eyes open immediately, and he looks from his bed to see a young Union officer dressed in the uniform of a lieutenant of infantry, the brass buttons carefully fastened on a dark-blue coat that is clean but rumpled. The brass insignia on his forage cap glows. In his right hand is a pistol, and his thumb is on the closed hammer. The pistol hangs easily at his right side. Otto thanks God that the officer is also a gentleman and is not waving the loaded pistol in front of his family. With his thumb on the hammer, he can put a bullet through Otto far faster than Otto could recover a pistol from under the pillow. Just behind the lieutenant stands Mary, with a look of horror on her face, and a three-year-old Lina clutching her leg and peeping around her dress.

Otto blinks, replying, "Yes, sir." Nodding, the lieutenant says, "Captain, you are under arrest. Get up, put on your uniform, and come with me."

Otto's tongue is dry and clings to the roof of his mouth as he does what he is told, selecting the newer uniform with fewer worn spots. He might be wearing it for quite a time. Putting on his overcoat, which he might need later in the year, Otto turns to the officer, asking, "May I say good-bye to my wife?"

The reply is "Of course, but I must remain with you."

Otto embraces Mary, enfolding her in the coat, whispering, "I will try to write, *libeling,* but it will be difficult to send out. Don't worry if there's nothing from me for a long time." He kisses her and then, picking up Lina, hugs her, saying, "Take care of your mother."

He stands at Charly's cradle for a long look and extends his index finger. It is instantly grasped. Otto shakes hands, mumbling, "So long, old-timer." Then turning, says, "Let's go, Lieutenant." The officer follows him, thinking his unwritten orders for civility to the citizens with German names is probably a good judgment. These people are decent, honorable, and not likely troublemakers if treated honorably.

Outside, Otto steps up to a horse that is held by one of two Yankee privates. He is not sure he can mount the animal after his illness and long period in bed. He tries to lift his left foot into the stirrup. The leg trembles, and he is far short of making it. His pride will not let him ask for help. He transfers the reins to his right hand, and using his left, he lifts the leg far enough to get the foot into the stirrup. He leans against the horse and inhales the odor of sweat and leather. Taking the reins back to the left hand, he grabs the saddle with his right and, with a command of stubborn will, kicks down with his left leg and up with his right and pulls on the saddle at the same time. It is not a graceful mounting, but he is on the horse. Now he instructs himself sit straight up and show these Yankees how a man can properly sit a saddle even if he is disabled with yellow fever.

The young lieutenant mounts another horse, and the party starts out of town on the road to Saluria. *What an irony,* thinks Otto as he observes the brilliant sunshine on the puffy trade-wind clouds, the scattering of color from the wild flowers, and their sweet aroma on a gentle breeze. *My life is collapsing, I'm ill and going to prison, and the world puts on its most beautiful display.*

Otto, turning in the Union saddle, asks, "How did you know where to find me, Lieutenant?"

"Not everyone in Indianola favors the Confederate side, Captain. One of your neighbors sent a message to us that you were home."

Otto is taken aback; he assumed that all Indianola was against the Union. Appalled at his own naivety, he asks, "And who would that be?"

"You know, Captain, I can't possibly tell you that. Just keep riding."

* * *

In Saluria, Otto prepares to dismount, knowing that his legs long confined to bed may simply give up and let him fall. Pride gives him the spirit necessary to swing his right leg clear of the saddle and down to the ground. There, his knee feels like jelly, and the muscles on the inside of his leg burn. Taking a firm grip of the saddle, he lifts his left leg clear of the stirrup and sets foot on the ground. Leaning against the horse, he prays for strength as his knees tremble. The Union lieutenant is enough of a gentleman to give him a minute before he asks, "Do you need assistance, Captain?"

"No, sir. The yellow fever has left me weak, but I believe I can make it." Standing free of the horse, he moves slowly, with much shaking at the knees. The more he moves, the better things work.

After a short walk, he stands in front of the desk of the major, who commands the troops occupying the dock area. The officer says, "Captain, you appear to have been ill. Is that why you were here at home?" Otto replies that he is recovering from a severe bout of yellow fever.

"Where was your station?"

"Virginia Point in Galveston Harbor."

"I'm not surprised that you caught yellow fever. Galveston is a pest hole of epidemic. What we are going to do is put you on a ship for New Orleans. You are fortunate there is one at the wharf now. You won't have to spend a night in that cage of a jail you people built at the fort."

Scratching out a brief note, he calls his orderly, saying, "Have Captain Schnaubert escorted to the schooner at the wharf and turned over to the ship's captain."

* * *

When the schooner leaves the dock, Otto stands in handcuffs on the deck and looks toward Fort Esperanza. How different things look from a new perspective. At this short range, the fort is extremely threatening. He can see the muzzles of six twenty-four-pounders pointed out at him and the vacant embrasure where the gun that he took had lain. He ponders the dynamics of the situation if the fort were firing at him. It would be just over one second after the flash before the shell would arrive. The guns would be pointed at the rigging, and the shell would arrive at deck level. The fort could not miss hitting something aboard the ship at this short distance.

When the schooner clears the bar and turns for its voyage to New Orleans, Otto is summoned to the captain's cabin. He finds a youngish man who says, "We are at sea now. If you give me your word of honor that you will not try to escape, I'll have your chains unlocked, and you may have freedom of the ship on deck. Of course, if you try to escape, you will drown. That would be inconvenient for me, but much more inconvenient for you. What do you say?"

Appreciating the easy humor, Otto replies, "Of course. I would not wish to inconvenience a gentleman such as yourself. You have my word."

The captain chuckles and offers a cup of coffee. They talk for a while, and Otto finds he is the only prisoner on board. As cargo for New Orleans, he shares the ship with three barrels of pecans, two hogsheads of molasses, and twenty bales of cotton.

It is strange to see the Texas coast from the other side, the side that he hated for three years. It is true as Will had said: at three miles offshore, the low coastline disappears at times. The water is a different color, not the gray-green of Matagorda Bay, but a beautiful bright green that glistens in the sunlight.

The captain shares his dinner with Otto, and the conversation turns to their homes and the war. The Yankee captain is from Connecticut. "I'm glad to say that the war has not come near my home and family. It must be very difficult for you to be repeatedly invaded and yet on the fringe of the main conflict in the East."

"The German people in Texas were initially against the war, but your blockade made our lives so miserable that the opinion shifted 180 degrees. Those of you that I have met are mostly kind and decent people. Sometimes I wonder why we are fighting each other. How did it come this far?"

"That is a good question. In my view, it would be all right for you folks to determine on a state-by-state basis whether you have slavery. But you cannot secede from the Union. Without the Union, America would be just like central Europe, a bunch of arguing and fighting states."

Otto's knowledge of the squabbling among the states of Germany lends respect for this view. "Doesn't it strike you as strange that you, a Yankee, are indifferent on the issue of slavery, and I, a reb, am strongly opposed to slavery as a crime against humanity, and yet, we both agree on the sad prospect of disunity? I think it shows that good men can look at the same situation and reach quite different conclusions."

* * *

When the ship reaches New Orleans, Otto is met by a sergeant and two troopers from the occupying force. The easy camaraderie of shipboard is replaced by a severe air of distrust as he is escorted on the short walk from the dock to the prison on Rampart Street. The clean odor of the sea is replaced with the stench of a city under occupation. At the prison, he signs in, spending two nights in a cell. The food is adequate, but he misses the freedom to walk about and stretch his bed-ridden muscles.

On the third day, he is escorted to the office of the prison doctor. The room has a strong odor of alcohol and a faint stench of chloroform. The doctor's uniform jacket hangs on a peg behind the door. He wears a white coat over the dark gray of his long johns underwear so out of place in the summer heat of New Orleans. The doctor asks him to undress and begins a cursory physical examination. Noting the looseness of Otto's belt and the color of his skin, he asks, "How much weight did you lose with the yellow fever?"

Otto wonders that his ill health is so apparent. He answers, "I think about thirty pounds, but I had gained some back while I was home with my family."

"Lie down on the table." Otto obeys and is subjected to a careful series of thumps on his chest by the doctor's index finger, applied with a careful listening to the result. The doctor rises, saying, "You can get up now and get dressed." He turns to complete some paperwork and, when Otto is dressed, says, "Captain, I think you have an enlarged heart. You seem to be recovering from the yellow fever. I am going to transfer you to St. Louis We have a hospital at Gratiot Prison there. They have excellent doctors and will provide fine care for you." What he thinks to himself is, *If this one is going to die, I'd prefer that it not be on my record at the prison here.*

* * *

Once again, Otto boards a Union ship, but this one is quite different. It is large with huge paddle wheels on each side amidships. A tall smokestack emits a dark stream of smoke as the ship clears the dock and turns up the Mississippi River for St. Louis.

The captain refuses his request to walk on the deck but agrees that he might sit on deck chained to the rail. In this fashion, Otto watches the green banks of the river pass by and cargo loaded on and off at stops along the way. It begins to dawn on him what a huge commercial viaduct the river is. The loss of Vicksburg in the preceding year is a greater tragedy than he thought. Now the Union has control of this great artery of commerce, and it is denied to the Confederacy. The western portion of the Confederacy is effectively severed from the eastern part.

* * *

At St. Louis, he transfers under guard to the Gratiot prison and hospital. This impressive three-story building is painted white with barred windows open to the summer breezes. The hospital occupies a wing by itself in the same building. Escorted up the stairs and through the hallways, he marvels at the equipment and supplies in evidence, realizing he has become accustomed to old and worn equipment and an absence of key supplies. The Confederacy appears tired and worn like himself, and here is the Union, strong and well supplied. His spirits sink.

The following day, Otto is escorted to the hospital wing and the surgery of a doctor who, looking at him, asks, "What is your problem, Captain?"

"On the trip up from New Orleans, my feet and ankles have swollen. I feel tired and weak."

The surgeon repeated the physical exam given at New Orleans. When this is complete, Otto dresses and sits at the doctor's table. "Captain Schnaubert, I am sorry to say that you are a sick man. Your heart is enlarged. This has caused your circulation to be sluggish, and the result is your swelling and fatigue. You must avoid heavy labor and any shock or stress. I will make out application papers for you to be exchanged. It will be a few weeks before that decision is made. That is probably good, as I'd like for you to be here for observation. I'm having you transferred from the prison to the hospital. We have good food here, and that may help you, but this is something from which you cannot recover."

* * *

That night, Otto lies in his bed. His mind will not give up and allow him sleep. He is amazed at the kindness of the Union surgeon. He is sick, not just the yellow fever. He could recover from that, although it might take time. His heart is going bad, and there is no cure for that. First, it is malaria, then yellow fever, and now his heart. His health is broken, and here he is in a Union prison with a family to support in Indianola. This malaise continues for hours until he lapses into a broken sleep.

In the morning, he is served an excellent breakfast with a real hen egg. He marvels, how long has it been since he has seen anything except occasional duck eggs at the fort? Fortified with this favor, he sharply commands himself to stand up and make the best of what he has. It does not occur that he has made the same speech on several occasions to his men. Still fortified with the speech, he asks for paper and a pencil. Addressing the colonel in command of the prison, he promises on his word of honor that he will not attempt escape if he can be allowed to walk about the town for a few hours. The fresh air might even aid his health. Surprisingly, the permission is granted.

The walk aids his health but not his spirit. Everywhere, he sees the bustle and energy that he associates with prewar Indianola. Remembering the commerce on the river, he knows now that the war is not winnable for the Confederacy. The Union will triumph. It is simply a matter of time. Returning to the hospital, he writes a second letter, stating that he is tired of the war and requests a parole. Two days later, a notice comes that he will be exchanged at Red River Landing in the vicinity of Baton Rouge. That will take place as soon as arrangements can be made. This exchange happens on July 22, when he begins the slow journey home, catching wagons when he can.

* * *

The two wounded men in the wagon with him make Otto feel shame over his self-pity. One has an amputated right arm and the other a healing but frightful wound to his face. Both are exchanged along with him and are now headed home. He notes the insignia on the forage cap of the one with the single arm and asks, "You were in the Eighth Texas infantry?"

The man replies, "Yeah, I was. Then I joined Waul's brigade and went on that trip into Louisiana."

Otto ventures, "I was commander of Company B in Hobby's Eighth. Did you know a captain Bletchley who was also in the Eighth and joined Waul?"

This question elicited a grunt and "Yeah, you know he was killed at Yellow Bayou? A sad little fight."

"What happened?"

"You know Bletchley, brave—not too bright. He came in late on the campaign. Was gonna make a show—tried to attack the Union troops in a cane break. Got shot. His men were not too keen about it. They just turned 'round and left him. The breaks caught on fire. That's the last anyone heard of him."

Otto ponders the paradox; he hates Bletchley, but that is a sad way to go, wounded and abandoned by your own men to die alone in a fire. The man yells for the wagon to stop. Getting down with one hand, he says, "I'm off here to go to Wharton. I hope you have a good trip."

Otto waves. What could he say? That man is not going to have a good trip in postwar Texas with only one arm.

CHAPTER TWENTY

Mary breaks into tears when she sees Otto at the door. "Oh, *Gross Gott*, you're home. I've missed you so and prayed and worried about you every night. And now you're here. Oh, *danke Gott, danke!*"

Lina looks very serious and advances slowly. Then with a rush, she grabs her father's leg and buries her face in the grimy gray material. Otto is speechless, his throat clenched so tightly no words will form. He turns his head from side to side and reaches down to hug Lina in one arm, Mary in the other.

She leads him to the bed, removes his worn boots, and covers him with a blanket, even though it is still summer. How he has changed! His face is tanned but drawn with a legion of tiny wrinkles where she remembers smooth skin. His lips are split with small bloody scabs, telling of his exposure to sun and wind. He has lost some weight, but the overall effect is one of extreme fatigue. She listens to his breathing and knows that he fell asleep without even speaking. There is much wifely work needed to restore this man.

"Frances!" Mary cries. "I've got to get some things for Otto. Can you mind the house and the kids?"

"Of course, do you want Lina to go with you and help carry sacks?"

"No, I want her to sit by and watch Otto. There won't be a lot to carry. Now, Lina, you will be his nurse and watch over him to see if he needs anything." Lina drags a chair to the bedside and sits staring fixedly at her sleeping father.

* * *

Mary returns in less than an hour with a beef roast, some potatoes, onions, carrots, and a bag of red beans. The beans go in a pot to soak with a pinch of baking soda. She goes to the bedroom where Lina sits with a serious expression, reporting, "He's very quiet, Mommy. He's done nothing but sleep. He has not even turned over. Charly made a lot of noise, but that did not wake him."

"Lina, you're a good nurse. One day, you'll have a husband of your own, and you'll know how to care for him." She takes the chair from Lina and silently watches the sleeping Otto.

Frances prepares the usual supper of fried cornmeal mush and bacon that evening. Looking at Mary, she says, "Don't worry if he does not wake up till tomorrow morning. I looked in on him, and he's breathing regularly and quietly. He's just plain worn out. I have seen Will sleep for sixteen hours." Then with a smile, "Of course he had other reasons to sleep that long."

"I looked in his coat pocket, Frances. There's a paper in there that says he was exchanged on July 22 at someplace called Red River Station in Louisiana. That was almost three weeks ago. He's been on the road that long. Who knows what he had to eat or where he slept." Mary stands up. Tears fill her eyes. She walks to the back door with her apron held to her face, crying silently. Lina rushes from the table to hold her mother's leg and console her. Nurses must be strong and help people. They do that even if grown-ups are strange.

* * *

In the morning, Mary fires up the kitchen stove, drains the beans, and sets them in a pot of fresh water on the back burner. Finding a large iron pot in the cabinet, she fills it with the roast, vegetables, and a little water, setting the covered pot on the other burner. She thinks, *That will take care of Otto when he awakens.* For the rest of them, she fixes the usual cornmeal mush as a start of the day. When it begins to puff, Frances and Lina sit and eat in silence. Mary has no appetite and puts her mush in Lina's bowl.

The timing of the roast is good. Otto stirs around noon and rises to go out to the privy behind the barn. On the way back, he stops on the porch to wash his hands and face in a bucket of water. When he enters the kitchen, he's able to smile weakly at Mary, wrap his arms around her, and say, "God, I love you, *Liebschen.* It's so good to be home."

"I thought you'd sleep forever, but I know you needed it. If you're hungry, there's something for you on the stove."

"Hungry? Mary, you can't know how hungry I am. The Yankees treated me well, but for three weeks, it's been catch-as-catch-can, and most times I did not catch at all."

Mary pulls out a chair for him at the table and puts a cutting board on the tabletop, setting the pot of beans and the Dutch-oven roast in front of him. She proudly cuts a slice of the beef and places that on his plate, scoops up the vegetables and beans to fill it to the edge. Otto's eyes grow wet as he looks at this lovely lady, and blessing the Lord, he begins to eat. His stomach cannot hold as much as he remembers. Stopping periodically, he talks about his travels to New Orleans and St. Louis and answers the inevitable questions.

"There are still a lot of Confederate army units in east Texas, so sometimes I could catch a wagon that had delivered supplies and hitch a ride for a few miles. Many of the units were reluctant to give supplies to someone who was on parole. Fortunately, a few took a more Christian view and handed over some of the tad ends."

"Were you able to get anything by way of forage?"

"We stretched things out with a few fish caught while waiting for the ferries at the rivers we had to cross. There's not a lot of traffic now, and the ferry men just seemed to go home and stay there. They did not want to take us across and not be paid. 'Course we did not have any cash. But they'd let us on board for free if there was a paying passenger going the same way."

"Oh, what a terrible time you have had, Otto."

"Don't say that, Mary. The ones that had a terrible time were the wounded and disabled. Many were on crutches and doing their best to make it home. I'll tell you, I felt fortunate when I saw some of them."

"There's not much to tell about Indianola. After the Yankees left, things have been quiet, and a few more shops closed. We had a couple of severe storms. What did you do on the road when it rained?"

"Sometimes we could not do anything but sit under a tree. Fortunately, in that storm with so much wind, about two weeks back, we found an abandoned farm and slept in the barn. That old barn groaned in the wind, and we sat on the windward side so if it fell over, it would fall away from us."

Lina listens carefully and quietly. Fathers are strange. They do strange things in a world that is even stranger. Nurses have to know about the world. She will have to think about this.

* * *

After a week of Mary's care, Otto feels the need for a walk downtown to stretch his muscles and see what Indianola looks like. The wharf area is a wreck with more buildings burned than he remembers from the day they shelled the Union fleet. On Water Street, he passes storefronts that are boarded up. One he remembers sold women's hats, ribbons, and thread. Mary shopped there for supplies in her seamstress work. He remembers her talking about the store's owner. She had excellent taste and was so enthusiastic about the future of the town. In her view, Indianola would become a bustling port to the West, and her share of this tidal flow of money would make her rich. The boards across the doorway told of one dream that had died in the wake of the blockade and the war. A walk up the street reveals dozens of tombs for the dreams of merchants.

* * *

Otto prospers under Mary's care. He is careful not to mention his heart problem, as there is nothing she can do, and it will only worry her. When two weeks pass, he reaches a decision. His presence at home is eating deeply into the money available to Mary and Frances. Further, he has no way to furnish extra rations to them. He is not receiving his pay. Of course, he might not get paid even if he is on station, but the only solution is for him to rejoin his company in Galveston. After some thought, he explains this to Mary. She denies that he is a drain on the budget but finally says that if he feels he must go, she will support his decision.

Together, they pack a sack for him with his canteen and a small iron pot. Mary insists that he take some beans and cornmeal even though he expects to draw rations at supply depots on the road. Searching in the barn, he finds a stout wooden rod that will serve as a walking stick. With two blankets rolled together, slung over his shoulder and fastened at the opposite hip, he feels ready for the trip.

Lina feels that fathers are even stranger than she thought. When they get to the place where they are going, they just turn around and go back where they don't want to be. Someday, when she has learned how to write, she will keep a journal about these things.

* * *

Otto, stopping at the Confederate States Army office in Indianola, shows his exchange papers and asks to draw rations so that he can rejoin his company in Galveston. The orderly remembers his capture in May and. with the papers, is glad to furnish ten pounds of cornmeal and five pounds of beans. He further says there is a small steamer that is going to Texana today and gives him a pass for the trip.

Otto is delighted to find this assistance at the very start. The steamer trip is interesting. He is familiar with the land route, but the view from the deck of the boat is subtly different. He sees the location where his guns were emplaced at Lavaca and pictures the problems of the Yankee ships facing his cannons. For a moment, he feels sorry for the Union gunners trapped here with no chance to maneuver. Then recalling the bombardment of Indianola and

Lavaca, he reverses that sorrow and wraps it around the casualties his unit suffered at their hands.

The boat stops briefly at Lavaca, which looks more demolished from the bay than it did from the land two years ago. The voyage continues to Texana, which is the head of tidal action on the Lavaca River. Here he thanks the boat's master and takes his bag ashore to find the army office.

The sergeant at the Texana depot reviews his papers and says, "The road direct to Columbia is well traveled now with wagons going in both directions. The movement of troops and supplies has changed the traffic patterns, making a primary road out of that old trail. You can simply wait here in the office until a wagon on the route stops to pick up mail or dispatches." This view proves to be optimistic, but three days later, he is on a wagon loaded with corn on its way to the Columbia Depot.

* * *

The wagon driver is a fount of information and happy to have a passenger to unload it on. Otto learns that it has been a good year for corn. "It ripened early, and that was good, because there were only the slaves to pick it and do all the dryin', shuckin', and strippin'. That took longer than usual, but there is the corn as you can see." Sack after sack of it lies in the wagon. Otto learns much more than he cares to know about corn farming, but it counts for mile after mile on the road to Columbia.

The next day reveals a good year for cotton. After that, it is a good year for sweet potatoes; and by the time that the status of the kitchen garden came up, he can see the buildings of Columbia. The driver pulls into the army depot, saying, "It's been real interesting talking with ya. Hope yer trip to Galveston goes well."

Otto let his ears rest before going to the supply sergeant's desk. He is surprised that the man remembers him from the year before. The exchange papers and his trip to rejoin his company brings out additional rations and the advice that there will be a wagon tomorrow on its way to Fort Green. Otto does not know where his company is, but that is as good a destination as any.

* * *

Otto sits that night on the banks of the Brazos River, cooking his cornmeal mush and beans and recalling the times he was here before. Those were winter and summer, in good health and poor. With all the trees along the river, it is beautiful, but full of bugs when the sun goes down. His cook fire helps to keep the bugs at bay. After supper, he buttons his shirt sleeves. Sleeping with the blanket wrapped around his head, he makes it through the night with a minimum of bites.

The clerk's advice is correct. The next morning, there is a wagon carrying corn to Fort Green, and Otto is aboard. This driver is an army corporal who has spent the last six months in the forts at Galveston Island. Otto thinks this is a chance to catch up on events he missed while a prisoner with the Yankees. Unlike the driver that brought him to Columbia, this man has almost nothing to say. Otto finds that the man has a German name and speaks limited English. Switching to German, he learns little more except that he man is from Saxony and is very tired of this war and being bitten by mosquitoes. *My god,* thinks Otto, *there is nothing worse than a melancholy German.* After a little thought, he laughs. *What am I?*

The wagon pulls up to the gate of Fort Green. Otto thanks the driver and asks the guard if he knows where Company B of the Eighth Texas Infantry is located. The guard replies, "Here at Fort Green, sir."

"And do you know where Company A is?"

"Just a moment, sir." Turning to the man in the guard shack, he asks, "Where is Company A of the Texas Eighth Infantry?"

After a minute, the answer comes, "Over on Virginia Point."

Otto produces his exchange papers and explains that he wishes to rejoin his company, asking to report in to the fort's commander. After a short conference, the sergeant in the guardhouse salutes, saying, "Captain, will you please follow me?" They walk the short distance to the commandant's office, where the sergeant confers with an orderly. He asks for the papers and disappears behind a door. In a moment, the door opens, and a friendly major that Otto remembers from Virginia Point appears with a smile on his face.

Otto salutes, saying, "Captain O. L. Schnaubert, reporting to rejoin Company B, Eighth Texas Infantry."

The major, returning the salute, says, "Schnaubert, I'm glad the Yankees turned loose of you. Your company, under the command of Lieutenant Beyer, is over by the north embankment. However, you were on sick leave when you were captured and on the road for the last month or so. I'd like for you to check into our medical station here and let the surgeon have a look at you. But first, let's sit down while you tell me about your tour with the Yankees."

They sit in the major's office for a half hour while Otto relates his experience in detail. The major is particularly interested in the situation in New Orleans and St. Louis and the traffic on the Mississippi River. Finally, he rises and, looking closely at Otto, says, "When the doctor releases you, stop by so we can talk again."

Outside, he is escorted to the medical station and introduced to a surgeon with gray hair and captain's bars who smilingly says, "Please take off your shirt and sit on the table here."

Otto recalls the procedure at the hands of two Yankee doctors and two Confederate doctors and knows beforehand what the response will be. The doctor, completing the examination, says, "Captain, you have an enlarged heart. You appear to have recovered well from yellow fever and to be eating well since your exchange. I would not recommend that you resume command of your company. There is a lot of stress there, and that will be hard on your heart. However, I think your company would benefit from your presence and your advice. Consequently, I'm recommending that you rejoin your company, but not in the commanding position. I understand that a lieutenant Beyer holds that position now. Will that be any problem for you?"

"No, Beyer and I are on the best of terms. He's a fine young officer. He was my first lieutenant for a year, and we shared a tent in that time. Your arrangement will work out just fine."

"Good. Now I'd like to keep you here for a couple of days for observation and to finalize my exam."

Otto rejoins his company two days later. Beyer asks him to share a tent, and there are smiles of welcome from the troops. He arrives at his second home.

Chapter Twenty-One

February 1865

Otto leans against the leeward side of the deckhouse on the small sailboat that runs between Virginia Point and Bolivar Point. It is uncomfortable out in the cold wind with spray coming over the deckhouse, but on the small boat, he feels better where he can see the horizon and get some feel for the movement of the craft. There is a thumping sound as the bow strikes another wave and a swishing sound as the spray comes over the rail. The odor of cold salt water is bracing, even if chilling.

This trip is his third run from the location of his company to the hospital on Bolivar Point, first from Fort Green and then from Virginia Point. Each time, his health would improve in the hospital, and then he would return to duty with his company, and it would go downhill. Beyer has completely taken over the company. Otto is being kept on in recognition of his extensive artillery experience and as a courtesy to his past standing.

He feels the heel of the boat ease off as they came under the lee of Point Bolivar and knew they would be alongside the dock shortly. When the mooring lines are made fast, he stands slowly, with much effort. Walking to the companionway, he smiles and thanks the helmsman, wishing him a good return trip. A medical orderly is on the dock to pick up the mailbag. His uniform is worn but clean, and his blond hair is neatly trimmed. Otto recalls him from the previous trips. If this shuttling back and forth continues, they might become good friends. He responds to the orderly's salute with "Good morning, Sergeant. I like your hospitality so much that I thought I'd come back for a while."

"Good morning, Captain. We have a room for you that has a nice view of the approaches to Galveston Harbor. You can watch the blockaders and the blockade runners. Sometimes it's a good show."

It is only a short walk from the dock to the hospital. He comments to the orderly, "I don't see as many people coming and going as I remember from previous trips."

"That's because the yellow fever epidemic is tapering off. Thank God for that. This was the worst year we have had. You know we were completely filled up here last summer, and the army took over a hotel in Galveston and turned it into a quarantine hospital. I don't recall if you were here then, Captain."

"No, I was enjoying a cruise at the expense of our exalted enemies, the Yankees."

"Where did they have you?"

"In St. Louis. It was a very nice facility, and the doctors were both efficient and courteous. Your food is good here, but theirs was like I remembered before the war. I'm not trying to recruit you, just giving them their due. I have to give you folks your due also. You have saved my neck twice now. I thought I'd see if you could do it a third time."

"All right, Captain, stop telling funny stories, or they'll think you're in too good a shape to admit here. After they let you in, I'll come by, and you can tell me the stories then."

* * *

After the familiar examination of chest thumping, ankle poking, and general survey, Otto is led to the room, which the orderly promised. There are four beds. Three have their mattresses folded back with bedclothes on top. The forth, placed by a window overlooking the bay, is completely made up. He could clearly see Fort Point and further down the island, Redoubt #3, where he had been stationed when his company first arrived in Galveston. He lies back on the bed, thinking this might prove interesting. Before he could think twice about it, he is asleep.

Supper proves to be several cuts above that at Virginia Point. He enjoys ham, sweet potatoes, rice and beans, and a cup of corn coffee with ample sugar. Clearly, the hospital has a different supply line than the regular army. Even the water tastes fresh and clean. Within an hour after supper, he sleeps again, this time through the night.

* * *

Otto awakes with an improved attitude but extreme fatigue. He lies back on the pillow and gazes out the window at the approach to Galveston Harbor. Although this is named the Bolivar Channel, Point Bolivar is distant from the channel and only lightly armed. The main artillery coverage is from Fort Point, where the ships must pass close to shore before entering the harbor proper. The orderly might be correct; there could be interesting sights from here.

Later, he dresses and walks to the mess hall to see what is available for breakfast. This includes bacon, hominy, and cornbread, definitely a cut above Virginia Point, and this cook knew how to make cornbread almost up to Mary's class. Lord, he missed her and Lina and Charly, not yet up to the crib-rattling stage.

Thinking of home, Otto is startled to see that a young captain, also a patient at the hospital, sat opposite him. His complexion is a poor color of light gray with a tinge of yellow. His dark hair is thin but combed back neatly, and his beard is tinged with gray that seems premature compared to his active brown eyes. The man smiles and introduces himself as from Company K of Eighth Texas Infantry.

"That was Ireland's company, how is he doing?"

"He's doing very well. It would be hard for me to imagine him doing any other way. I'm not up to that standard. I caught the yellow fever this past summer. Having a hard time recovering, but this hospital is a good place to try it."

"Where is your company stationed? Mine is currently at Virginia Point."

The man thinks for a moment, saying, "Redoubt #3. I think you have been there." Then with head lowered, "Things are as bad in

Galveston as they have ever been. General Hawes is in charge of the town, and Prince Magruder is in residence." He pauses, looking out the window, then continues, "Military law does not sit well. The citizens talk as if they'd rather have the Yankees come back. There's very little love for the Confederacy in the town." He shifts position in the chair then begins again, "This past winter, there was no firewood in the city, and people tore down all the wooden buildings that were not inhabited. Just to burn and keep warm."

"Isn't that a bit of irony? Magruder, whom we all welcomed as the savior when he recaptured Galveston from the Yankees, is now the hated boss of military law in the same city."

Otto feels glum about the spirit in Galveston but thinks it's time to change the topic. "I saw in an old Houston paper that the U.S. Congress abolished slavery in January and sent that out to their states for ratification."

The man looks up and fiercely says, "It's about time. I could never stomach the idea that this war is fought to preserve slavery. The men who do the actual fighting don't have slaves." That view was just fine with Otto.

He asks, "Anything interesting with the blockade runners? I understand they're not as active as when I was over at Redoubt #3."

"That's right. But there was an interesting set-to last month when the *Susanna* made it into the harbor. She went in broad daylight right through the blockaders. They shot her up pretty bad. Funnel shot off, bow all smashed. But she made it. I understand the captain misjudged his approach in a night fog, and sunrise found him right in the middle of the Union fleet. They did not dare pursue him once he was under protection of the guns at Fort Point. The *Susanna* made it, but I doubt she'll go out again. By the time repairs are finished, this war's gonna be over."

"You think so? Is it that close?"

"I'm not on the inside, but when I was over on the Island, I'd see the big brass. They were sorta looking over their shoulders and whispering together. You know, Sherman has pretty well torn up

Georgia. That Grant fella has shown he's not as timid as the other Yankee generals. Yeah, I think it's close."

The discourse seemed to tire him, and Otto, thinking that rest was the better choice for both of them, says, "I'm a little tired. I hope we can continue this tomorrow." Back in his room, he again looks across the harbor and reflects on the dozens of sharp encounters that took place there in the last four years.

That night, out on the horizon, there is a sharp orange flash of light, followed a minute later by another. This is on the Yankee side of the bar and too far away for sound to be heard clearly. Some ambitious Southern skipper is trying to make his fortune out of the exalted prices forced by the blockade. Well, he thinks, *I wish him success and minimum damage.*

* * *

The Houston paper brings the news in April that Richmond has been occupied by the Union army and the Confederate government evacuated. Two weeks later, a special edition announces that Lincoln has been assassinated. Again, Otto sits in the mess hall with his friend from Company K. He ventures, "I'm stunned by the Lincoln killing. What were they thinking? This will only make the Yankees that much harder on the South when the end comes."

"Yeah—the end's pretty close, isn't it? I wonder where Jefferson Davis is tonight."

"Wherever he is, he's a lonely, bitter man."

This speculation was interrupted by one of the hospital staff who says, "Gentlemen, we are starting to evacuate. Will you please come with me to get your hospital discharge papers?"

* * *

It is the reverse of his landing two months ago. The small sailboat is at the Bolivar dock, preparing to go to Virginia Point and Fort Green, where Otto's company is now stationed. The contrast to his landing is sharp. He is in much better health, but the atmosphere is somber. Men move quickly back and forth between the hospital and the dock. No jokes or funny comments, simply a morose and hurried pursuit of the necessary tasks.

After a short sail, he watches the unloading at Virginia Point with no particular emotion. Everyone seems convinced that the end is near and tries to make the best of the final days.

The small dock at Fort Green comes in sight. He stares at the underside of the causeway that he has used twice to enter and leave Galveston Island. These things always look different from the other side. Is the war itself like that? What would he feel if he were a Yankee about to win this four-year contest? He steps ashore and walks to the commander's building to report in.

* * *

Gen. John Bankhead Magruder meets with his staff in the office on Galveston Island. Word has just been received that Jefferson Davis was captured near Irwinville, Georgia. Prince John relays this information to his staff, concluding his remarks with the advice that it was now "every man for himself," adding, "Take whatever you can carry."

Magruder personally considers an offer from the blockading fleet that if he surrenders, they will assure him good treatment and transport to New Orleans. He weighs this against what he might receive from the Galveston citizens or those of west Texas if he stays in place. He chooses to board a blockade runner headed for Mexico. They have a civil war going there and possibly could use an experienced senior officer.

Chapter Twenty-Two

May 25, 1865

Otto climbs to the highest point of Fort Green, at the mainland end of the causeway to Galveston Island. The sun, just setting, casts a red tinge on the heavy ground fog. At the other end of the causeway, a flag pole is visible as a short rod rising through the top of the fog. Hanging limply from that pole is a Confederate flag, which the fog slowly obscures as it rolls in from the Gulf and covers the island. The sun sets, and the red-tinged fog turns a dirty gray. At his feet, the boards of the causeway are as wet as if it had rained. The flag appears an omen. Tomorrow will be the formal surrender of the Confederate forces in Texas with the future masked in a dirty gray.

His emotions are in conflict. For a year, he has known in his heart that the cause for which he fights is hopeless. This day is partly a relief that the end has come. But he mourns the loss that the last four years have brought—the death of friends, the destruction of much of his hometown of Indianola, the loss of his own health. Men do not cry. He simply gulps air spasmodically with his eyes closed. No tears come.

* * *

The night before, Otto walked down the line of mules and found Maggie. She recognized him with a snort and a nudge of her nose against his chest. Scratching behind her ears, he recalled the surveying effort for the new fort, the mule railway, and occasions when talking gently, he had gotten an extra effort to pull a gun carriage out of mud or sand. She had carried him round trip between

Galveston and Indianola. With luck, they can do it again. He cut Maggie out of the line, led her away, and staked her behind his tent.

Now, under a gray overcast, he saddles and loads her. He rides down to the gate of Fort Green. There is no guard. The soldiers were mustered out two days ago. Otto thinks he would be safe even if there had been a Yankee guard. Maggie's rump was unbranded, showing that she has never belonged to the U.S. Army. Grant at Lee's surrender allowed officers to keep their personal mounts. If stopped, he will simply say she was his personal mount; he has ridden her for four years.

They start down the road traveled twice before. He feels tired even though it is only midmorning and knows he could not make it home without Maggie. His thoughts are interrupted by a cry of "Captain Schnaubert!" coming from a group of men standing at the side of the road. In recognition, he says, "Sergeant Rochow, I see we both made it this far. Are you headed for Indianola?"

"We're all headed for Indianola." Otto then recognizes the seven other men from Company B; *former company*, his mind says. This thought is quickly corrected by an inner voice that says, *No, it's your company, and it always will be for both you and them.* Forcing a smile, he says, "I think Maggie here will carry part of your load."

Clearing the space in front and behind the saddle, he helps the men place four pairs of bags there. Sitting straighter, he says, "Men, we will go the reverse of our march from Lavaca to Galveston eighteen months ago. I expect we can use the same campsites we used then. If you don't have a walking stick, speak up when you see a likely sapling along the road. We will wait while you cut it. Let's go home."

In three days, they reach Columbia on the Brazos River. Otto thinks it would be wise to call a day's halt and do some fishing to supplement their rations of cornmeal and beans, which he drew from the depot there. The supply dump is essentially open to any soldier. No papers needed, no records kept. Just take it before the Yankees get here.

His fatigue lessens in the day's rest, and the march to the Colorado River begins. When they reach Wharton, he again needs rest and uses the same excuse. This time, he feels that he did not quite recover. The next leg is about three days to the Navidad River. There, some of the men run out of rations, and fishing is an absolute necessity. The next leg is only two days to Indianola. That night, he sternly tells himself they will make it.

A brief stop is made in Lavaca. They are recognized as the artillerymen who drove off the Yankee ships. This brings the gift of several loaves of bread from the townsfolk.

The business district is a sad sight. There has been no lumber to permit reconstruction, and the city looks much as it did the morning after the bombardment two and a half years before. The railroad has been torn up for over five miles, and no rails or ties are in evidence.

The group of nine begins the last twelve miles to Indianola with heavy hearts and light stomachs. Otto rides ahead and asks a farmer to take a wagon out, meet the eight men on the Lavaca Road, and haul them to Indianola. When this is done, he turns to go home himself.

* * *

Reaching home, Otto sits for a few minutes in the saddle, not sure he is strong enough to dismount without falling. By the time he decides that he can get down without injury, Mary sees him and runs from the kitchen. He stands for a minute, knees shaking, leaning against Maggie's side with Mary holding him tightly; tears running down her cheeks.

"You're home, *Liebschen*, thank God, you're home. I have missed you so. Then sensing his weakness, she says, "Let me help you to the kitchen. Maggie can take care of herself for a while." Otto makes it to the kitchen and slumps into a chair. He can't bring himself to tell Mary that he is so weak. Women were supposed to depend on men for their strength, and here he is with not enough strength to take off his boots. What a sad excuse for a husband.

Mary has learned watching Mutti that men are not as strong as they try to appear. The last thing a lady should do is let out they knew that secret. She forces a smile, saying, "I'll bet you haven't slept for days. Let me help you to the bed and take off your boots." This is accomplished, and Otto falls asleep, confident that Mary does not know how sick he is.

Mary unsaddles Maggie and leads her to the barn. The mule does not object when she removes the bridle and pulls down fodder. She returns to the kitchen, considering the problem of getting Otto well. The solution seems to be food, rest, and a visit from Dr. Reuss. With this decided, she gives away to her own fears and sits on a chair with her head on the table and cries quietly into her apron.

* * *

Otto awakens early and, lying in bed, considers his problem. He has a family to support. Mary and two children need food and shelter. He is not sure that he can work at anything. He has not been paid by the army for several months. And the last payment in Confederate dollars is now worthless. His situation seems hopeless. Rising, he walks to the barn where Maggie stands to meet him. She starts to nudge him with her nose, stops nervously, then backs up in the stall with wild eyes and shuffling hooves. This person looks like her rider, but he does not smell like her rider at all. This man has the strong, bitter odor of fear.

PART VII

Chapter Twenty-Three

June 1865

Dr. Reuss arrives at the house the next day, summoned by Frances Moore who tells of Otto's sad condition and Mary's fear. Greeting Mary and Lina, who stands quietly in the corner of the kitchen, he says, "Good morning, and good morning to you, Charly." The alert two-year-old stands on the kitchen floor, pushing on the rails of his vacant crib and making it rock back and forth. "Your family looks good, Mary. Where's the head of the household?"

"In there, Doctor," replies Mary, trying hard to speak clearly over the constriction in her throat. She leads him into the bedroom where Otto lies back on a pillow.

"Well, Otto, I have seen you look better. Unbutton your shirt and let's have a look at your chest." Reuss makes the same finger-thumping examination that the Union doctors performed, feels his forehead, opens his mouth, looks at his tongue and throat, rolls up his cuffs, and pokes the swollen ankles. Then pausing for a moment, he purses his lips, saying, "Unless you do something stupid, you're not going to die this week, but you are going to have to adopt a new style of living. You have an enlarged heart, and that's the primary problem. This means no physical labor for you. Also, you should avoid anything that gives you emotional stress. I expect that the surrender and the ride has been a huge stress. That is your second problem right now." He folds the covers over Otto's legs.

"Mary will take fine care of you, but I'm worried if you can take care of yourself. Maybe you could put away your idea of being a surveyor for a year or so and use your God-given talent as an artist. There are some people that came through the war with a little money. I will see if I can convince any of them that we have a real European master here in town and that maybe their home would look good with one of his paintings over the mantle." Lowering his head a little, he continues, "What do you think?"

"Reuss, I don't know what I think, but I'm listening to you. Let me have a few days to consider that?"

In the quiet of the night, Otto repeats in his head the lecture on doing with what you have instead of crying for what you want. It seems to work a little, and after a hot sponge bath and a good dinner, he sleeps for twelve hours. Mary begins to worry at the length of his sleep, but Frances wisely points out that he is breathing steadily and appears relaxed. When Otto does awaken, he is hungry and, on finishing a hearty breakfast, talks with Mary about their finances. She smiles proudly, saying, "You recall the $500 you sent me?"

"Yes, but that was Confederate—it's worthless now. We don't have anything to live on."

"Erdmuthe got it changed into U. S. dollars. There are seventy-five of them in our account. Frances and I both receive money for soldier's families. That pays the rent. Our sewing pays for the food. What's this about nothing to live on?"

"You mean that if I did sell a painting, that money would go into our savings?"

"That's exactly what I mean."

Otto has another slice of cornbread and a cup of corn coffee. He thinks silently and then walks out to the barn to use the privy and pull-down fodder for Maggie. She watches him approach warily and, when he is near, puts out her nose to take a tentative sniff. Yes, this is her rider; he looks right and smells right. She puts her nose against his chest and gives a gentle nudge. This is not a bad place for a mule to be.

* * *

In July, the Union army sends troops to occupy Indianola. Parole officers set up tables on the sidewalk downtown and begin to officially complete the surrender. On July 7, Otto saddles Maggie to ride downtown and sign two documents, the Parole of Honor and the Amnesty Oath. When these are completed, he rides through the business district to see what the town looks like after the surrender. No one tells him or any of the other Confederate soldiers that their amnesty also means they are disenfranchised and prevented from voting in future elections.

The business district is in worse shape than he remembers after the shelling in the fall of 1862. There is additional damage to the wharves and buildings. Those that were damaged in the shelling are now destroyed and the structure carried away for firewood.

Surprisingly, there is a beehive of activity where the long wharf had been. Instead of silence, there is a continued hum of conversation punctuated by an occasional louder command. The occupation army has a desk with a sign Laborers Wanted. Inquiring, he finds that the army will immediately rebuild the wharves and warehouses to permit shipment of supplies to the forts of west Texas. It is exactly as Shea and Runge forecast. Knowing that he could not stand up to the effort involved in construction labor, he asks, "Do you need experienced engineers for supervision of the construction?"

The young captain surveys him, sees the signs of illness, and says as kindly as he can, "No, sir. I expect you could do a good job for us, but we're bringing in our own engineers."

Otto returns the kindness, saying, "Thank you, sir." Then with a glance at the man's insignia, "Your Thirty-Fifth Infantry troops appear in good form, Captain. I look forward to the completion of the wharves and their operation again."

The change in the downtown area since his last visit is amazing. There is nothing yet in the warehouses or the stores, but the noise and bustle is overwhelming. He begins to feel the energy is back in Indianola. The future will bring prosperity for everyone.

* * *

There is no work for Otto that doesn't involve labor. When he arrives home, he finds that Mary has brought in the box with his sketchbooks and art supplies. Wisely, she has not unpacked it but left that task for Otto. He opens the bundle of brushes wrapped in oilcloth and tests them against the back of his hand. Surprisingly, they are flexible. He tries each one in turn, recalling their individual capability. He holds one to his nose. The faint odor of linseed oil sparks his memories.

The paints are in a small wooden box with a tight-fitting lid. Sliding back the lid, he looks for a moment at the small tin tubes, each about the size of his index finger. Tentatively, he pinches one. To his surprise, it is pliable, indicating the oil inside has not hardened. Thoughts of past paintings arise as he reads the labels: chrome yellow, viridian, madder, zinc oxide. It all seems so long ago. Could he possibly start again?

Each sketchbook is held shut with a colored ribbon that identifies it and keeps the pages flat. He opens the one with the green ribbon. Thumbing through, he sees pen and ink sketches of Saxony done when he was a student in Chemnitz. The work seems to be that of another person. He finds himself thinking, *He's not too bad.* That brings a laugh. He opens the small one with the red ribbon and finds his sketches from New Mexico and west Texas. The next one is larger and has a blue ribbon. It contains sketches of Indianola and Lavaca. There is also a portrait sketch made prior to an oil painting. Finally, a sketch of Mary appears. His throat catches as he feels her beauty. Looking up, he compares it with the real thing and thinks she is now even more beautiful. Tears form in his eyes. He hastily attributes that to the illness.

There are blank pages at the back of the blue book. Looking across the kitchen, he sees Lina, watching him with a serious expression. He smiles, and she responds slightly. "Good lady," he says. "Would you pose for me?" Seeing that she does not know the word, he begins again, "Lina, would you sit in the chair here by the window?" She does. This man is her father. Mother has said so.

Fathers are strange. You must do what fathers tell you even if you don't know why.

"Lina, I want you to sit still in the chair. Can you do that?"

"Yes, Papa."

Otto takes a heavy carbon pencil from the box and starts to sketch. Across the kitchen, Mary finds tears in her own eyes and turns away, appearing to start supper. Otto is not pleased with his sketch, but Mary is delighted. Lina asks herself if she really looks like that. She finds her mother's mirror and ponders the matter.

After supper, Otto rummages further in the box and finds the pieces of a small stretcher and a rolled scrap of canvas. Using his knife and borrowing a meat hammer from Mary, he cuts and stretches a small canvas. He then sizes it with the zinc-oxide paint. Tomorrow, he will paint a portrait of Lina.

* * *

The portrait does not please him. The figure is well placed in the frame, the clothes are acceptable, but Lina looks stiff and not at all childlike. However, the skin colors are good. He is just not loose enough. A small voice says, *What did you expect after four years of not painting?* Stilling the voice, he says, *That can be fixed.* Going to the ship chandlers, he buys three yards of canvas and a quart of white paint. Back at the house, he cuts, stretches, and sizes another canvas. Lina watches this with grave concern. The smells are strange but interesting. Charly laughs and shakes the crib rails.

The next day, Otto starts again. He does not notice a return of spirit and concentration that has been missing for months. Mary sees it and, reverting to her childhood days, crosses herself, muttering a "Hail Mary." Otto paints again. The portrait does not please him. The composition is fine. The clothes look like cloth with folds in the right places. The background provides the right contrast, and the skin is radiant and childlike, but the total effect is not a child.

Later in the month, he is through two and a half yards of the canvas. With a stack of portraits nailed to the kitchen wall, the man who taught painting before the war looks carefully at his most recent work. He cleans a small brush and, with the tiniest load of white, adds a few highlights to nose and chin. The child is alive!

Lina is still not sure about all this, but Mary is. She splurges slightly on the food budget and prepares a stew of Matagorda oysters with real butter and two shakes of hot sauce. Otto sleeps soundly with a warm stomach in front and a warm Mary in back.

* * *

Frances takes the portrait of Lina to show Erdmuthe, who carefully considers it and, going to her attic, returns with a frame that matches the size of the painting. They fix the painting in the frame with small wooden wedges made from toothpicks and try it on the wall in Mutti's parlor. It is splendid! Taking the painting, down they walk to Reuss's house. Mrs. Reuss answers the door and asks them in, commenting on the painting, which she immediately recognizes as Lina.

Mutti has a simple question: "How can we get the people of Indianola to recognize that we have a great European painter in residence and have their children remembered in his art?"

Mrs. Reuss calls up the stairway, "John, there's something here you must see." There is a sound of steps in the upstairs hallway and then on the stairs.

"Mary and Mutti! What a pleasure, in fact a double pleasure." Then turning to Mary, "How is he?"

"I think this painting says it better than I could. He's practiced for weeks, and he's finally pleased himself." Saying this, she holds up the painting for inspection.

Reuss takes the painting to a window and, after a few moments examination, says, "This is wonderful! I remember that he used to teach painting, but I don't recall having seen any of his work. This could be the best thing possible for his recovery, Mary."

Mutti asks, "John, Otto needs to have the encouragement that would come from people buying his paintings. That would allow him to feel he could buy art supplies and continue doing work like this. Now that shipping has resumed, there is money coming into town. How can we convince the holders of that money that we have a fine European painter here and their family should be recorded in his art?"

"You have just convinced one of them right here. I'd like for Otto to do two paintings, one of Mrs. Reuss and I, a second of the whole family. That should keep him busy awhile. When we get those hung, we'll invite some of the moneyed aristocracy over to show off our paintings."

"What a marvelous idea," says Mutti. "I'm doing peach fritters tonight. Would that would fit with your dinner?" This was directed to Mrs. Reuss, who acknowledges it would fit beautifully.

"Well, I will send some over with Frances. The new crop of peaches is in, and they really are sweet."

* * *

It goes much as Erdmuthe envisioned. Otto does the portrait of Dr. and Mrs. Reuss first, recalling the two years that he and John spent together at the fort. Several people later remark on the depth that Otto has put into his painting of John. When the painting of the family is finished, Mutti's plan works its wonder. Having a family portrait done becomes a basic step in the assent of the Indianola social ladder, and Otto is the recognized master of the art genre.

* * *

Frances enters the tiny house with little William on her hip and glances at Mary. The sad expression causes Mary to ask, "What's wrong?"

"I'm sad and happy at the same time. You know Will got a job on a Morgan ship as soon as he signed his parole. Well, he's found a nice house for us to rent. He says that, with one baby in hand and another on the way, we just need more room. It's a nice house, but

I hate to leave you. We have been so happy here. Will you be all right?"

"Otto and I will be just fine. He has a small payment to begin a painting, and there will be more when he finishes it. So we'll make out just fine." Noting Frances's expanded waistline, Mary says, "You forgot to tell me that you had another baby on the way! What wonderful news."

Frances, hugging Mary and seating William at the same time, laughs with tears in her eyes. "I'm so mixed up! There's too much happening. Will wants to move this Saturday. Do you suppose that's too soon?"

"It will be just fine, but you know Otto won't be able to help, much as he'd want to. He's just not supposed to do heavy work or lift things."

"Will says he's going to get Williams to help. He was in Otto's company too, and he's working in the engine room on the same ship. All that we need is for you folks to keep the kids in check. We don't have much. We will get a wagon to haul it in just one trip."

"I'll get my brother to bring in a wagon from the farm. It's the least we could do for your new house."

When Saturday comes, Will brings Williams over to where Otto is sitting, saying, "You remember Williams from the company at Fort Esperanza?"

"Of course, how are you, Williams?"

"I'm doin' fine, Mr. Schnaubert, but I've got to say thanks to you for clearing those charges when I did a stupid thing about goin' on that boat. The guys that went aboard did just fine. I was just too scared."

"Williams, I'm glad it turned out as it did. Let's simply not worry about it ever again. What are you doing on the ship with Will?"

"I'm working the engines. That's my specialty, you know. And although it's hot inside the engine room, it's a place where I feel at home. I'm fortunate to be working again so quick after the war."

Mary's brother sets the brake on a wagon pulled by Maggie, who seems to have benefited from her new home. There is not a rib showing, and her coat is brushed clean. The long ears turn from one side to another as her head swivels to take note of everyone at this gathering. Otto is greeted with a snort and a dip of the head. Clearly, mules lived as well at the Noll farm as they did "in the old country."

It takes very little time for Frances's few belongings to be loaded. Otto and Mary, waving, watch the wagon disappear from sight as it turns the corner. *That*, thinks Mary, *is the end of an era. Now there is just the four of us.*

CHAPTER TWENTY-FOUR

Fall 1866

Between the army, in its rush to equip forts in west Texas and J. P. Morgan in his desire to build a shipping and rail route to California, money pours into Indianola. Steadfast conviction in the promise of the town leads the citizens to pour their money into construction and infrastructure. There is bustle, energy, and a sense that anything is possible. The universal belief—as Indianola grows, wealth will come to all who work and save and, above all, believe in that future.

In the year from September 1865 through August 1866, the imports are 80,389 containers of general merchandise; 62,306 containers of groceries; 10,099 barrels of flour; and 2,063 bags of coffee beans. Evidencing the construction boom are imports of 2,210,235 feet of lumber; 1,002,229 shingles; and 2,412 kegs of nails. Even the import of ice, cut from northern lakes in winter, is resumed for summertime usage. It is delivered as far as Victoria.

A total of 486 vessels clear the port with exports of 9,342 cotton bales; 8,935 bags of wool; 69,451 hides; and 40,028 goatskins. Indianola is the second-largest port in Texas and well on its way to bigger and better things.

* * *

Mary hears the knock on the front door and wonders who could be calling in the middle of the morning. Opening it, she finds Frances Moore, excited and bubbling with news.

"Mary, it's too good to be true. You know that Mutti lives just one house up the street from Will and me?" There was no pause for an answer. Frances continues, "Well, on the other side, the house is now up for rent! It's really a nice house, and we can be next-door neighbors. It would be like it was when we shared the house. You have just got to come see it."

"Frances, I don't know. Otto is selling a few paintings, and things do look up, but could we afford it? Well, I don't suppose it would hurt just to go look." They did, and the house was all that Frances said.

That night, Mary opens the topic with Otto. She is surprised to find that his success in selling a few painting has completely changed his outlook. He points out that Lina could have her own room, which will be important for her when she starts school next year. Then laughingly, he adds, "It will be important for us right now to have our own room." They agree to go look at the house the next day. Later that night, a sleepless Mary silently prays, "Oh thank you, dear Lord, thank you."

They rent the house and join the community of Mutti and Frances.

* * *

As fall comes, Christian French has what his brother George describes as a "capital idea!" The brothers run a saloon on Water Street that is showing a profit, but could use a pickup in sales. Christian elaborates, "On the fifth anniversary of our victory at Fort Washington, we could hold a party at the saloon for all the artillerymen that fired on that Union sloop on December 7, 1861. First round on the house, then a few plates of hard-boiled eggs and pretzels—then watch the sales of drinks mount up."

Handbills are printed and placed in stores around town. Invitations are mailed to all the officers, both commissioned and noncommissioned. Even the *Sangerbund* agrees to sing a few Christmas carols. The word spreads quickly, and the response is positive.

*   *   *

On the fifth anniversary, at least thirty former artillerymen assemble in the saloon. The occupation army disapproves the request to fire off a small powder charge in the middle of Water Street to initiate the proceedings. But after some thought, they allow the celebration to take place indoors. It is as Christian had seen it. After the free round and pretzels, drink orders mount, and conversation becomes animated.

Otto, speaking over the mounting noise, asks, "Reuss, have you heard anything of Shea?"

"Not a word. You know he was in the command in San Antonio when the surrender came. He made it to lieutenant colonel. I thought he would come down and try to start a shipping company. Maybe he saw the way it was going with the Morgan Line coming back in and taking over the shipping. You know Morgan had sold almost all his ships to the Union navy at the start of the war. Then after the surrender, he bought 'em back and started his New Orleans to Indianola service. Smart man. But that's no place for a paroled rebel colonel."

"What's that about the Morgan Line?" asks Will Moore.

Reuss, turning to see who was inquiring, says, "Will! I understand you are in line for congratulations—first mate! Let me buy you a drink."

"I'm still aiming for captain, Dr. Reuss. Maybe you could buy me a drink then if you're still of a mind. Have you heard anything about Major Ireland?"

"He went back to Seguin and started up his law practice again. You know he was mayor of Seguin before the war. I expect we'll hear more of him in the political arena, He's an impressive man."

"I do know that. You recall I was in his company briefly before I transferred to the *Carr*. I felt like I was a traitor to leave Captain Schnaubert's company, but I must say, I learned a lot from both of them."

Otto turns Will around, saying, "You may not know it, but I learned a lot from you. I'm ashamed to realize that I never said you were my eyes and brains when it came to ships."

Will asks, "What about Major Vernon? You know, I see you almost every day, but I don't think to ask until there's an occasion like this."

"He went back to Madisonville in Madison County and has become a painter, just like me. Isn't that something? If someone forecasted that five years ago, we would have laughed. Looking back, he was one of the best commanders we had."

Otto slaps Will on the shoulder and moves to stand with a familiar face, saying, "George Rochow, do you remember our surveying tasks for the military?"

"Oh yes, indeed I do. I'm teaching school now, Otto. I often think about that practical application of mathematics and my brief experience with it."

"I'm glad to know that school is in the hands of a knowledgeable and responsible person like you. My oldest is going to be in your school next year. A German upbringing gave me great respect for school and its importance to a free country. But when your own kids reach school, that idea truly comes home."

Later that evening, the *Sangerbund* did a rendition of "Stillegenacht, Heilegenacht." Nearly every eye in the room was wet, remembering Christmas Eve 1863 and the sound of that carol drifting over the prairie to lonely pickets after the great Christmas dinner contest.

* * *

For Indianola, the economic flood continues in 1867, and nearly all boats are floated. In that year, imports of lumber are up 300 percent, shingles 130 percent, and coffee 500 percent. Exports of cattle are up 50 percent, cotton 70 percent, and general merchandise 900 percent.

But there are setbacks. A fire burns the post office, the customs house, David Lewis's drugstore, and three other mercantile establishments. There is immediate consternation, but the firm belief in the future of Indianola prompts a rebuilding. The city purchases a new fire wagon that can use the endless water supply of the bay in any future accident. The end result is merely a pause in the steady progress and growth.

In June, the Methodist Church building, where Otto and Mary were joined, is finally paid off. In the same month, a yellow fever epidemic starts, and Will Moore's father dies. A mini reunion occurs at the funeral.

Reuss is appointed to the school board, and in the fall, after yeoman service in the epidemic, he writes a survey on the effects of yellow fever on urban populations. Through it all, the city prospers. The dream is being confirmed.

* * *

In 1869, a seminal event occurs. Canned beef has long been an Indianola export product. The problems and limitations are well known, but the proximity of the huge Texas cattle ranches and the solid shipping connection to New Orleans make the business profitable and sales grow steadily.

The new trial product is refrigerated beef, butchered in Indianola, refrigerated ashore, and hauled in refrigerated ships to New Orleans. Due to a fortunate coincidence, the time delay in transport and the temperature at which the beef is held approximate the process, which will later produce "aged beef." Consequently, the reception in New Orleans is instantaneous. Indianola's "refrigerated beef" becomes a gourmet product in a city known for its cuisine. Within a year, shipping is regular to both New Orleans and New York. Another boat has floated, confirming the beliefs of those who see prosperity as the birthright of this city.

Chapter Twenty-Five

Fall 1871

It is only natural that there should be a tenth anniversary of victory at Fort Washington. This is brought forward by the brothers French in a new location. Christian has opened his own bar, the Office, on Main Street in a choice location close to hotels, restaurants, and the courthouse. George has opened his bar as part of Villeneuve Hall, established by Casimir Villeneuve as the city's center for political meetings and other performing arts. The hall is two doors away from the Office.

The anniversary program is much as that of five years earlier, but the talk is heavily on achievements of Indianola and its prospect to be the leading port of Texas. Shortly after the "round on the house," Otto proposes a toast to the new streetcar system. "Indianola takes its place among the cities of the world with transportation from the residences to the arts and business district on new clean cars pulled by strong mules." He then follows that with a toast to the railroad, which now connects Indianola to Lavaca and soon San Antonio.

This is followed by Reuss, who toasts, "The completion of the telegraph service, giving us connection to the news of all America."

George Rochow, schoolteacher and Reuss's son-in-law, toasts, "The installation of gas lighting that will permit reading under adequate light in the home, or pleasant conversation in places of business or entertainment such as we have tonight."

Christian French offers, "A toast to Capt. William Moore of the new steamship *Emily*, copper sheathed and bronze fastened, the trimmest ship operating out of Indianola."

William offers, “To the ship *Bolivar,* which, this year, initiated direct steamship service between New York and Indianola.” He follows this with a second toast, “To the regular shippers from the East that bring us ice from wintertime ponds so that we can have ice cream in the summer.” This last refers to the confectioner who expanded his trade in 1871 to include iced sodas and ice cream.

Otto turns from his participation in the toasts to comment to Reuss, “Did you hear that General Magruder died in Galveston this summer?”

“Yes. I talked to a doctor I know there who said it was trouble with his heart.”

“You know, he was not as bad as I thought at the time. In many ways, he saw what was coming and did his best with what he had. He was certainly the most creative general that we had.”

* * *

Not all had been roses in 1871, but it would be bad manners to bring it up. There had been a hurricane in the summer. It did not hit the city directly, but it had a severe effect on Lavaca. The storm surge was the highest in memory, but that just meant some businesses were flooded. The Office, where the party was now in process, had two feet of water in the barroom. Christian passed it off that “the floor needed washing anyway.” All the mules and cars of the streetcar system were moved to the high elevation in the north of town and spent a day of rest.

Everyone revels in the 300 percent increase in population from the prewar level. There is no note that many of the houses built to accommodate this influx are at lower elevations than the established residential area to the north of town.

* * *

At the age of ten, Lina enjoys school, where she excels. In her own room at home, she can read or study without bother from her younger brother, Charly. She often helps her mother with the new baby, Arthur. Babies are strange but better than younger brothers. Why couldn't she have a sister? They could sit and have girl talk.

Charly tolerates school and enjoys recess and, most of all, trips to his grandfather's farm to see cattle and horses and an old mule.

Mary and Otto revel in having a room of their own.

CHAPTER TWENTY-SIX

Summer 1875

Indianola prospers. The population is now eight thousand, four times its prewar level. Railroad service is regular and connects with stagecoaches to San Antonio or via another railroad to Houston. One can buy a ticket with connections to California by stagecoach or direct to New York by ship.

The city has six opulent hotels and four gourmet restaurants, one of which boasts "New York and Parisian experience." One can buy a grand piano, with a choice of Steinway or Chickering, and the latest sheet music to play on it. Fine furniture is available from two new stores. Nouveau riche people of exquisite taste can be satisfied without leaving town.

In the Office, Christian French and lawyer Fletcher Stockdale muse on the progress of Indianola, "Time was when I was one of two lawyers in town, now there are six."

"And doctors too, I remember when Reuss was the only sawbones in town. Now we have four of them."

"Well, there's one place where I could do without growth. That's taxes. You know in '67, the tax rate was fifteen cents per hundred dollars evaluation. Now it's two and a half dollars per hundred. That corrupt bunch around Governor Davis should have been tarred and feathered, not just run out of town." The Carpet Bag Era ended in 1874 when President Grant refused to support Davis with U.S. troops.

The county courthouse has a new jail and a vault with brick walls sixteen inches thick to preserve the vital records. Indianola definitely has surpassed Lavaca as a Texas port.

The conversation at the Office continues as Reuss joins Stockdale and French. "We were just talking about you two and the increase in doctors and lawyers. What are you havin'?"

"Some scotch whisky and a little of that new soda water. Well, one growth we don't need is crime. Did you hear about the shooting on the boat? They brought me these two bodies, both shot in the back—asked if they're dead. Any fool with one eye would know the answer to that, but I filled out the form anyway on March 11, 1874, for William Sutton, and another for Gabriel Slaughter, poor guy was just standing there. It was Sutton the Taylor brothers were after."

"I heard that Sutton's wife was right there when it happened."

"Yeah, she identified the Taylors and the two corpses. It was a straightforward ambush."

"I understand she put up a $1,000 reward."

"Yup, she's a brave lady."

Fletcher decides to change the topic, asking, "How's your son, Reuss?"

"He's gonna be out of med school next year. I'm looking forward to taking him into the practice. The way the town's growing, we need a new doctor. And if I don't get home quick, I'll need my son to patch me up when Mrs. Reuss clobbers me with a broomstick." This brought a big laugh; everyone knew she was the last person in town to do any clobbering, and the doctor was the unquestioned master in his own home.

Stockdale pulls his gold watch out of its pocket and, laying a bill on the bar, heads for the door. Christian picks up a towel and continues drying glasses.

* * *

At fourteen, Lina is in high school and finds that she is good at math. Her father helps in this and is duly proud of his daughter's accomplishments. Little Charly will be in high school next year and looks forward to that elevated status, well beyond Arthur, who isn't even in school yet. Older girls are strange, but younger brothers are a real pain. Taking his pocket knife out on the back porch, he resumes the whittling of a wooden figure of a horse.

Maggie is retired and enjoying John Noll's experiment of growing barley in saline soil. It is even better than alfalfa fodder, but does not quite equal the fresh rye grass at Agua Dulce Creek.

In the dynamic prosperity of Indianola, there is one problem in that hot summer of 1875: no rain has fallen for a year. Farmers pray for a soaking rainstorm. No one thinks of the adage, "Be careful what you pray for, God may give it to you."

Chapter Twenty-Seven

October 1875

The captain of the steamer *Caribbean* in the Atlantic Ocean west of Africa slams the door to the bridge and rubs his head with a towel. Seawater runs from his sou'wester coat. The deck tilts at thirty degrees from vertical before making a shuddering stop and slowly righting back to ten degrees. A green sea comes over the bow and strikes the bridge a violent blow. He shouts over the screaming wind, "Prepare to transfer steering to the after wheel." A second helmsman is sent to the alternate steering station, and on a signal to the bridge, steering is transferred. The captain grabs the log. He and the helmsman abandon the bridge and take up station at the more shielded location. It was not too soon. A half hour later, a huge wave strikes, smashing the bridge windows. The next wave carries away the starboard bridge wing. Within ten minutes, the entire bridge structure is swept away. The captain enters in the log:

> *September 6, 1875—Tremendous hurricane . . . shipped sea . . . knocked away the bridge, lamp room, boats, skylight, and later, shipped tremendous sea carrying away boats, engine stopped . . . Carried away the man at the wheel.*
>
> *September 8, 1875—Starting with one engine for St. Thomas.*

Meanwhile, 1,500 miles to the west, Christian French finishes drying a glass in the Office and turns to greet a customer. The cut and color of his suit proclaim "salesman." Christian is pleased. That group brings a large business to his saloon on Main Street close to the downtown hotels. "Good afternoon, sir, how can I make your day more pleasant?" asks Chris.

"I think a double shot of Kentucky bourbon would be a good start."

"Would Medley's 12 suit you?"

"Ah yes, splendid . . . a true sippin' whiskey." The description is illustrated with a small sip and a sigh of satisfaction. "Tell me, sir, what is going on in your good town?"

Chris introduces himself as the proprietor of the Office and asks the reason for the question.

The salesman, after another sip, replies, "I asked for reservations for five nights at the Excelsior Hotel and was welcomed for four nights but told they were completely booked from the thirteenth on. I tried five other hotels and received the same reply. I have been traveling here for a year and never have seen anything like this."

"Oh," replies Chris, "it's the trial. Bill Taylor is being tried for the murder of Gabriel Slaughter and William Sutton. It begins on the fourteenth, and people from all around have planned to come and see it. Biggest event since the railroad was finished."

"Sounds interesting. Where can I get a place to stay?"

"You might try the boarding house on Travis Street. It's just two blocks over. Big yellow house, but there's no sign out front."

"Thank you, Mr. French. I'll try that place." With a large sip and matching sigh, he says "Good day," and walks out onto Main Street.

* * *

The hurricane, passing between Haiti and Jamaica, hits the tiny island of Navassa on the twelfth. The mayor of the local town barricades himself in the town hall when trees three feet in diameter are torn up by the roots. Waves break over the cliffs forty-five to seventy-five feet above sea level. The schooner *Serene* clears Navassa on the tenth and the brig *J. F. Spencer* on the eleventh. Both sail into oblivion when overtaken by the storm. It then passes over Cuba, exiting just east of Havana. By the thirteenth, the weather bureau in Washington is aware that a hurricane is active and telegraphs a warning to Mobile, Alabama. No warning is sent to Indianola as landfall is forecast much farther to the east.

* * *

The trial starts in Indianola on the fourteenth. With the courtroom packed, the crowd overflows the courthouse and into Water Street outside. When a recess is called, the traffic into the Office causes Chris to call his brother George to come over from the Casimir Bar and help him tend the customers. Snatches of conversation detail the progress of the trial.

"That's a tough-looking jury. I would not want to be Taylor tonight."

"The county attorney really laid it out, did he not? Said Taylor and his brother shot the two of 'em in the back, right there on board the ship."

"Did you see Taylor's face when the charge was read? Especially about the feud between the Claytons and the Suttons?"

Later the topic changes to "Where shall we eat supper?"

"The restaurant two doors down serves excellent Matagorda oysters."

"I'm going back to the Excelsior Hotel and then to the steak house on B Street. Why don't you join me?"

* * *

When they close at eleven o'clock, Chris and George count it their largest day's sales since the bar opened four years before. George marvels, "There must be upward of two hundred people in the hotels here just for the trial."

Chris counters, "Maybe a few more. There's a surprising number of families—Mom, Dad, even the kids. I would not have thought a potential hangin' would be so popular."

* * *

In the warm waters of the Caribbean, the powerful storm gains energy. On the fourteenth, the *Witch of the Wave* leaves Tuxpan, Mexico, and the schooner *Mabel* clears the mouth of the Mississippi. Neither is heard from again. On the fifteenth, the storm track changes when a high pressure area over the United States moves eastward. The track veers from north to northwest. Mobile is spared. Indianola's fate is sealed.

* * *

It is midafternoon of the fifteenth in the Office. The crowd from the trial has not yet arrived. The wind begins to blow steadily up Main Street. The door opens, and Chris turns to see Will Moore walking quickly up to him. "Afternoon, Will. I don't see you very often. How have you been?"

"I have been well, Chris, but I think that we got trouble, and I wanted to warn you. Thought maybe you could pass it on to a few of our old friends. It's this storm. I don't like the looks of the southeast sky and the way the wind's rising something fierce."

"Will, I have never seen you upset over a little wind."

"This one is different. There were sun halos this morning. I'm taking Frances and the kids over to Palacios where there's some high ground. Then the mate and I are going to put the ship out to sea and ride it out. I already warned Erdmuthe. She's gonna take the train to Victoria and stay with friends there. Otto and Mary Schnaubert and their kids are going with her. You have a lot of money in your stock here. I thought you might want to get it someplace safe."

"How bad could it be, Will? We're pretty secure here."

"You remember '71? The water came up into your bar then. I don't know how bad it will be, but I know it's gonna be worse than '71. I gotta go, Chris."

Chris calls George over, and they discuss what Will has said and debate closing as a prudent choice. On the other hand, there will again be record sales tonight and tomorrow. They decide to stay open. This decision seems correct when the bar rapidly fills. Snatches of conversation keep them up to date as they hustle to fill the orders.

"The county attorney really put it to ole Taylor, waving that big pistol."

"He's beginning to sweat a little. Did you notice? I think he remembers all the blood."

"And Slaughter was shot just for bein' there. Ain't that something? Not a part of the feud, just standin' there."

"The sheriff has got Taylor in control. You see that big pistol he's got? He ain't goin' to run."

Chris lights the gas lamps, and a cozy yellow glow gives a feeling of warmth and comfort. The rising wind seems safely at bay.

Across Water Street, Sergeant C. A. Smith at the weather station begins to share Will Moore's concern. The wind shifts over to the east. Staying on duty, he telegraphs Washington: "The wind continues to rise. Breakers are sweeping over the offshore islands into the bay."

After closing the bar, Chris and George feel less confident. They pack some of the more expensive liquor and move it to the second floor of the building.

* * *

At sea, the hurricane reaches its peak force the morning of the sixteenth, testing that force against the offshore islands. Fort Esperanza is eroded away by the breakers. Bombproof dugout, mule railway, and bridges all disappear. Upper Saluria is completely washed over by breaking seas. All of the houses are destroyed. Of the five Morgan Line pilots stationed there, four drown.

There are two lighthouses on iron foundations inside the bay. The keeper of the westward one feels confident that the iron foundations supporting the wooden house will prove solid against the storm. He reassures his alarmed wife when they first see breakers coming over the Matagorda peninsula. It is now too late to use the skiff that is tied outside. Looking, he sees that the skiff has its bow underwater. The storm surge exceeds the length of rope securing it to the supports. While he watches, a wave breaks white over the foundations, and the skiff disappears. Minutes later, a wave strikes fully on the southeast side of the house, breaking a window and causing the house to shudder terribly.

Taking his wife in his arms and turning her back to the storm, he watches in horror as spray comes through the window and blows horizontally across the dining room. A huge wave strikes the house, which shudders and tilts slightly. Minutes later, a second monster wave strikes. Boards creak and pop. The floor tilts, and furniture sweeps into a pile on the northwest wall. The walls tilt more as nails scream and are pulled from the boards they held for decades. There is a huge crash and sounds of broken glass as the light and lens fall against the roof and into the sea. He has just begun, "Our Father which are—" when the complete house and contents are swept off the bent iron foundations into the bay.

* * *

Indianola is next. By midmorning, seawater is running through the business district in a direction perpendicular to the bay shore. The rushing water tears out the foundations from the buildings of the business district. Opened bottles in the Office begin to float and clink against each other. The foundation shifts, and the walls creak loudly as nails are unseated. Then a loud crash occurs as the wall breaks open, and the building falls into the rushing water. Kentucky bourbon bottles that had traveled the Mississippi River and the Gulf of Mexico begin their final voyage into Matagorda Bay.

Just after 5:00 p.m., the anemometer at the weather station blows away. Subsequent estimates of the wind velocity are 140 to 150 miles per hour. By 6:00 p.m., the building between the weather office and the bay collapses, and a schooner anchored in the bay crashes into the back of the station, collapsing it in turn. The schooner is later found five miles away in the new lake formed behind the town. Sergeant Smith has wisely abandoned his post for the safety of the concrete courthouse, one of the few buildings that survive in standing condition.

People in the hotels have little chance. The foundations are undermined, and the structures tilted, sending occupants from their rooms to seek safety in the lobby. The lobby is found to be filling with water. The hotel guests start to climb back to their rooms when the walls tilt farther, and with the screams of nails, boards, and humans, the structure collapses into the surge.

By midday, the wharves tear apart, and masses of heavy planking surge through the business district. The huge mass of debris batters bodies of those caught in the hotels and restaurants, greatly complicating the later identification of bodies.

The peak storm surge reaches fifteen feet. The water, driven through the business district to a low area behind the town, forms a lake fifteen miles in diameter. At the peak, twenty million tons of water lie in this new lake.

* * *

The wind dies. A horrible quiet prevails. Briefly the sun shines. Some think they have survived.

Then the wind, which blew from the southeast to create that new lake behind the town, starts up from the northwest as the eye passes directly over. It blows water out of the lake back into the bay. Twelve new bayous are cut by this rushing flood, five of them through the business district all the way across the town from Powderhorn Bayou to the bay. Entire blocks are swept away in this flood. With the wreckage go the bodies of nearly all of the out-of-town visitors who came to witness the trial. Completely demolished are the six hotels, four fine restaurants, the Office, and Casimir Bar. Reuss's drugstore is simply gone.

On Main Street, Louis De Planque has his photographic studio. Next door is his residence, a neat two-story building with an attic bedroom. The inrush of the storm surge floats his studio. The waves drive planking into it, destroying thousands of glass plates. The recorded images of the people and the progress of the great postwar reconstruction are demolished. The residence lasts until the backwash begins. Its foundation is swept away, and the house joins the line of floating wreckage flowing down Main Street to the Bay. Louis and family are fortunately in Victoria and escape personal harm. The hurricane, effectively destroying the existing Indianola, seems bent on destroying also the record of its progress preserved in the thousands of glass photographic plates.

Approximately two-thirds of the homes suffer the same fate as the business district. Unfortunately, many are swept with their occupants into the bay and on into the Gulf. Ships approaching Indianola in succeeding days report planking, debris, and corpses in the Gulf beyond Pass Cavallo for many miles. Bodies are found on the beach for twenty miles. The dead are estimated at eight hundred, but this total is probably low as the number of out-of-town guests is not known.

Will Moore takes his sloop and his family to Palacios, where a friend will house them at his farm. Frances, in Texas housewifely fashion, felt she must take some gift to the house. She orders the mate to "get" her some mullet. This is different from "catching," which implies a rod and line. Mullet are ubiquitous in the bay and are usually "gotten" for bait but considered edible in a pinch. To "get" mullet, a circular net is used. It has weights around the periphery and lines that pull it together through the center. The net when thrown, with a rotating motion, opens up and falls on the school of mullet, which is fighting for pieces of torn-up bread. The net falls rapidly to the bottom where the lines are pulled together, forming a sack full of wriggling fish. The mate cleans and scales the catch, while Frances rolls them in cornmeal and fries them in bacon drippings. She feeds her family and the mate and takes with her a large plate of fish for the house that would temporarily be home to her and the kids.

Five days after the hurricane passes, Will Moore's wrecked sloop is found in the Saluria area. No one is aboard. Frances will not give up hope and returns to Indianola. She is proved correct two days later when Will and the mate walk into town, uninjured but chastened. He plans to have another ship built.

News of the catastrophe travels rapidly, and rescue efforts are launched from Victoria and Galveston. The train from Victoria is loaded with supplies, medicine, and helping hands. It must turn back when it finds the railroad track washed out for five miles from Chocolate Bayou to Indianola. The ships from Galveston face a similar problem, finding the wharves and warehouses completely destroyed. They return to their starting points or anchor in the bay and begin a slow off-loading using small row boats and skiffs.

The trial that lured two hundred people to their death has an ironical closure. Bill Taylor, the accused, convinces the sheriff that rising water will drown him in his cell at the courthouse jail if he is not released. He signs on his honor that he will not try to escape if freed. But when released, he steals a horse and makes an astounding nine-hour ride through the rising waters to Green Lake. There he leaves the horse at a livery stable and sends a note to the owner, saying where the horse can be found. He disappears into frontier Texas. He may be a murderer, but he is not a horse thief.

CHAPTER TWENTY-EIGHT

November 1875

Reuss is on the first train from Victoria trying to reach Indianola. He leaves his family, except Augie who is at med school in Galveston. The train reaches as far as Clark Station, ten miles from its goal. He finds the conductor, asking, "Why are we stopped?"

"The track is washed out about five miles from Indianola. We can't even get into Lavaca. We're going back and try something else."

"I'm a doctor. They need me in there. Is there some way I can make it even if the train can't?"

"You might find a farm and ask for a horse to ride in following the railroad embankment as far as it goes and then riding across the prairie where the track is washed out. I don't recommend it."

"That's a good idea. We passed a farm about a mile back. Will you stop there when you start the return?"

"I'll do that, Doctor. But I don't recommend it. You might check the supplies in the car ahead. Take anything you can use."

Reuss gets off at the farm. Leaving a letter to his wife and taking a bag of food and medical supplies, he hikes to the farm in search of a horse. The farmer is reluctant to part with an essential animal from his farm. Then in sudden recognition, he says, "I remember now. You're Captain Reuss of Company B. You fixed up the ship so them fellows did not get yellow fever. I was in Company A. You did not know me, but I thought what you did was real thought out. Here, you can take my horse, but you gotta bring her back and keep her safe, she's no young foal. Come to think of it, neither are you. Be careful, Doctor."

Reuss picks his way into Indianola and is horrified at the level of destruction. He finds a temporary hospital set up in the courthouse, which, minus its windows, survived structurally. He also finds one of the towns other doctors there, who is delighted to share the medical supplies. Reuss asks, “What are we doing about a morgue?”

“There is no building standing. We are laying the bodies out along the railroad embankment where Travis Street used to be. Crews are taking them out along the lake for burial. They are trying to keep an accurate list of names, but it’s difficult. Some of the people caught downtown among the wharf planking are completely beyond identification.”

“How many?”

“I have no idea. We’ve had about thirty die here, but that’s only a small fraction. I think we’d better get back to work. They’re bringing in some more from the houses up town.”

It is a day and a half before Reuss feels he can take the time to look at his own house. The mule streetcars are not in operation. The rails are either completely buried or lying in air, bridging one of the new bayous that cross the town. When he reaches the place where he thinks his home should be, he finds nothing but piles of random planks. Surely, he must be wrong. Then, turning, he looks for the courthouse and takes a cross-bearing on the root of the north wharf. He is about a block further to the west than he thought. When he finds the house, it has fallen into a new bayou over 120 feet wide. It is too dangerous to enter. His house, his books, and all their belongings, including Otto’s paintings, are simply beyond reach.

On the way back to the hospital, Reuss stops to view his drugstore and finds a worse condition than that of the house. The drugstore has simply disappeared. He has lost everything but his family.

* * *

When it is finally possible to return to the town, Otto finds that damage is much less in the area where they lived with the Moores and Mutti. The houses are at least standing, but roofs are damaged or missing completely. Nearly all of the windows are broken.

When Otto and his family reach their rented house, they find the wooden steps that led up to the porch missing. This mystery is solved when they spot a similar front step floating in a nearby pond. The wooden step is a well-made box, loosely fastened to the porch. When the flood came, the box simply floated away from the house. They retrieve the step from the pond and, setting it against the porch, enter the house. Lina rushes to her room, finding no roof overhead and all of her books soaking wet. She does not cry but fiercely promises herself that she will never come back to Indianola again. She believed in it and studied hard, and it has ruined all that she held dear.

Otto's response is nearly as complete. Ten years of paintings are buried in piles of debris or washed into the Gulf. When he tries to locate the shed behind the house, he finds that it is gone, and with it, his prized surveying equipment, except for the transit, which stays in the house. Well, he will likely not use it again, but it is an emotional loss nonetheless.

Mary finds some of her kitchen utensils inside the house. The beds, although water logged, will be usable when they dry out. But all of her pretty curtains are blown away, and the parlor furniture is ruined. The home that she has made is a wreck.

Charly is the quiet one. His carved wooden horses and cows all washed away through the flooded and broken windows. He cannot imagine his ranch and riding among the cattle to take care of them. He has spent so much time carving them, and now they are gone.

Arthur is simply thunderstruck. His books are soaked, as are his clothes. The baseball and the catcher's mitt are simply gone—somewhere out there in all that destruction they had seen on the way in. It is not fair—it simply is not fair.

Otto gathers his family together and tells them that they will move inland, as far as the railroad can reach—Cuero. That will be their new home. They will take all of their belongings with them as soon as they can be dried out. With their arms around each other, they each in their own way give up their dreams of Indianola.

Two-thirds of the population of Indianola follow the example of the Schnaubert family, transporting their dreams from Indianola to Cuero or Victoria.

Part VIII

CHAPTER TWENTY-NINE

December 1876

Christian French stands behind the bar of his new saloon drying a glass. The light of the gas lamps on the wall cast a warm and welcoming glow through the small room. It is not as large as the Office, his previous saloon, but it will suffice for the fifteenth anniversary celebration of the victory at Fort Washington. With two-thirds of the old-time settlers moved out of Indianola after the 1875 hurricane, he does not expect many attendees. The party will not aim to increase sales but rather to remember old times.

He turns as the door opens to admit Will Moore. Chris addresses him and asks, "What would you like for your on-the-house starter?" Will opts for bourbon, and while Chris pours, he asks, "How are things with your family?"

"You know, a full answer could take all night. We have five now. Frances finds her days full taking care of that brood. The oldest is twelve and looking forward to high school. He's old enough to work summers with me on the boat. He'll be a good seaman."

"Does Frances hear anything from her mother, Erdmuthe?"

"They write to each other about every week. Mutti has a little house now, next door to Mary and Otto Schnaubert. You know, there were so many people moved to Cuero from here that they named a new area Indianola Street. Mutti is sort of a gathering point for all the family kids."

"What do you think of that move by J. P Morgan?" asks Chris.

"Not much. That was a dirty trick this summer to force out his partners on the railroad and then stop train service out of Indianola. I hear that Ireland is trying to drum up a movement to revoke the land in west Texas that was deeded to him for starting the railroad. I would not work for Morgan now. Anyway, I have my own boat. It's not as large as the *Emily*, but it's a well-built sloop and adequate for coastal freight or fishing."

"Isn't that move by Morgan going to kill the freight business through Indianola?"

"It would, except that he started up again in October. It does put a question mark on the freight that was headed through here for San Antonio and west Texas. It may very well go by rail from Galveston. I think this town is going to become something else, maybe a resort where people come for fishing or bathing. I understand that's gotten to be pretty big in the East."

"Brother George is doing well in Corpus," says Chris. "He gave up the saloon business after the hurricane and went into a grocery store instead. He's doing all right. Corpus is growing a little, and he grows right along with it. Has anyone seen Dr. Reuss?"

"He's doing well in Cuero, opened a drugstore. He and his son, Augie, are in practice together. Henry Runge even opened a bank in Cuero. You know he moved to Galveston after the war and changed the name of his store here to Henry Runge and Co. It was a good thing for the town that the safe in his bank, with all the records and the money, survived the hurricane. The depositors did not lose a penny. Some of them started rebuilding right away from the money in that safe."

"Yeah, and others took the money and built in Cuero."

"Maybe that's why he opened the bank there."

The light outside dimmed as evening neared, and the gas light made the bar seem more comfortable and homey. The conversation continued for several more rounds, but the group of two reflected the reduced status of the town. They were those who believed their dream still lay with Indianola.

CHAPTER THIRTY

1876

The aroma of frying bacon permeates the kitchen when Lina Katlyn, washed up and dressed for school, enters and asks, "Where's Papa?"

"Don't you remember, Lina, he went to Indianola and brought home that old mule from Grandfather's farm yesterday? That was so he could ride out to his new job as surveyor for the state on the railroad? He left about six this morning, with that old transit of his in a box."

"Did he have something for lunch?"

"Yes, I fixed him a sandwich and a jar of hot soup. You don't think I'd let him go hungry, do you?"

"I'm sorry, Mama, I was just thinking about him out there by himself and hoping he'll be all right."

"He won't be by himself. His rodman and chainman are meeting him out at the shack where the right-of-way ends. They'll survey the next section of land for the state. I must say, he looked happy to be up on that old mule. I don't exactly understand why he has to do this, but he was happy about it."

Charly and Arthur tramp in, all ready for school. Before Arthur can speak, Charly announces, "I brushed that old mule until she shined last night. She remembered me from the time I spent on Grandfather's farm and gave me a snort and a nudge with her nose. When will Papa be back?"

"He'll be back for dinner tonight. Now eat your breakfast and on to school with all of you."

Out on the old right-of-way, Otto sits comfortable on Maggie's back and observes the thick growth of weeds that obscure the earlier work. It was abandoned when another railroad company went bankrupt. Now the work is resumed by a new company that wants its 640 acres of land for every mile of railroad built. He recalls how Ireland used to curse the railroads for stealing Texas blind. At the time, it did not seem to matter to him.

The pain in his left arm is surprising, but not severe enough to cause him to rein in the mule. The meeting point with his crew is probably a mile ahead, maybe fifteen minutes. He'll see about it when he gets there.

The feeling in his chest starts like indigestion but quickly develops to a sharp pain that causes him to rein in Maggie. He leans forward onto her neck and moves to dismount. His right leg gets over, and with a tug, his left foot is out of the stirrup. He hangs there for a moment draped across the saddle. The pain comes again sharper this time. He slides down the stirrup leather to the ground. Curled up on the ground, he emits a deep groan.

At the shack, the two assistants wait anxiously. It's evident Otto is late, and that's not like him. One of them suggests they walk back along the right-of-way and, after some discussion, decide that one will walk back and the other stay at the shack in case Otto shows up.

The one at the shack starts whittling on a pine limb, and after what seems like a long time, judged by the pile of shavings, he hears a cry from his partner who is running up the right-of-way and shouting, "Help, come on. Help me."

Together, they run down the track, finding Otto on the ground. They put him over the saddle and tie him in place. "Come on, we got to get him to Dr. Reuss as quick as we can." Leading Maggie, they start off down the track back to town.

Later, one describes it to a friend, "When we found him, there was this big mule standing right there and looking down at him. She turned and looked at us like we should help and stood stock still while we tied him in place over the saddle. Then she turned and started for town at an easy walk like she was trying not to jostle him."

"You took him to Dr. Reuss?"

"Yeah, Reuss said there was no hope. He was clearly dead. Then he mounted the mule and rode it over to Otto's place to tell Mary what had happened. We went to tell the state people that the survey would be delayed."

* * *

"Mary, there is no good way to tell you, so I'm going to be right up front. Otto has died."

"Reuss, it can't be. I just fixed his breakfast this morning, and I packed his lunch."

"I know what death is, Mary, and I'm terribly sorry. I think it would be good if Erdmuthe came over and stayed with you for a while. In fact, I can't think of anyone better. Shall I ask her?"

"What happened?"

"His heart just gave out. You and I both know that it had been coming for a long time."

"But it's so unfair. He was finally about to do what he wanted all along—to create something useful, a railroad that could serve people. The hurricane took his paintings, and now death has taken him before he could do what he wanted. It's so unfair."

"Mary, I have wrestled with death for all of my career. Sometimes I won, and sometimes I lost, but I have never seen death be fair."

* * *

Erdmuthe hugs Mary close and makes soothing noises that seem not to penetrate a shower of tears. The children make an untimely return from school with long tear-stained faces. Charly goes to the barn to see about Maggie. He brushes the dust from her. "I know you did all you could. You couldn't do more. When things settle down, I'll saddle and ride you back to Grandfather's farm. You can enjoy a long retirement."

Lina goes to her room and, holding a small Bible that Otto had given her, prays to a god who oversees bad things happening to good people. “I know we can’t understand your ways, but it seems terribly unfair to take a good father just when he is going to do the thing he wants to do and for which he studied and worked so long. Your will be done.”

Arthur sits in the kitchen and tries to console his mother. A hopeless task.

Chapter Thirty-One

1886

There is not a twentieth anniversary of the victory at Fort Washington. The survivors are down to just Christian French and Will Moore, who nevertheless drink a round together in memory of old times.

Christian is dreaming of a twenty-fifth reunion in August 1886 in the midst of a hot summer. It is not to be. On August 19, a hurricane strikes Indianola for the third time. The storm surge is at least as high as in 1875, but the final blow is a fire, which burns every building in the business district but two. Ironically, the fire is thought to have started from a broken oil lamp in the signal office, which was established to warn of hurricanes. The casualties are less than in the previous hurricane only because of the smaller population. This time, the dreams expire.

* * *

Will Moore's confidence in Indianola's ability to rise yet again leads him to buy up lots in the ruined city as residents have their grand Victorian homes disassembled, the boards numbered and shipped inland for reassembly in Victoria or Cuero. Will's confidence is misplaced. The county seat is moved to Lavaca, and the post office address is canceled.

Finally, he stands on the shore where the long wharf had been, knowing that Indianola is finished. A taught anchor chain stretches out into the bay. The chain holds no ship at the other end. Instead, a locomotive lies beneath the waves. It was driven onto the wharf to "hold it down" during the high winds. The wharf was undermined by the storm surge. The faithful locomotive continues to perform its last assigned duty of holding down the tracks, which were to serve an Indianola as the transportation hub of south Texas.

Will looks up the beach. All that defies the wind is the broken corner of the concrete courthouse. Bowing his head, he steps into the skiff to row out to his ship and leave for a new home in the small fishing community of Palacios. He looks inland. The tiny cemetery is just visible, already invaded by saw grass ruffled by a steady wind, unseasonably warm, and loaded with humidity. The movement of the saw grass causes a stream of sand, which moves to fill the crevices around the tombstones. The flat, treeless land reclaims the ruins of a city where once there were dreams.

EPILOGUE

Reuss's dream was to practice medicine with his son. This seemed to be achieved in full as Augie graduated from med school and joined him in Cuero. Death, his nemesis, claimed this son at age twenty-six. His second son finished med school and joined him in practice. Reuss lived a long and successful life. He and son won many struggles with death. Perhaps his success was the result of clearly seeing both his dream and his nemesis. The bodies of Reuss and his family lie in Hillside Cemetery at Cuero. The cemetery faces Reuss Street. Four generations have managed the Reuss Drugstore in Cuero.

Otto Schnaubert, less clear in the vision of his nemesis, was delayed in achieving his dream to build things of value and utility as an engineer. With his health broken, he achieved success as an artist. His health, the true nemesis, claimed him a year after the 1875 hurricane. It was through his daughter, Lina Katlyn, that his dream was finally achieved. She married Charles Dickerson, Erdmuthe's son. They had two sons, two grandsons, and a great-granddaughter, all of whom became engineers developing things of value and utility in the twentieth and twenty-first centuries.

Mary Schnaubert's dream of love and family was achieved with her three children and loving husband. She worked hard all her life, and the early death of her husband placed great hardship on her to raise the family. She provided excellent education for her children. In later years, encroaching blindness and rheumatism reduced her earnings as a seamstress, and she depended on her loving daughter Lina Katlyn for support. In the year 1910, she became one of the few widows living on both Union and Confederate pensions.

Lina Katlyn completed school through the diligent efforts of her mother. Her husband, Charles Dickerson, a volunteer fireman, died in a crash on the way to a fire when he was thirty-eight and Lina was thirty-four. She took over the management of the family hardware business and ran it skillfully enough to afford a college education for their two youngest boys. She lived to be eighty-four and graciously willed her savings not to her children but to her grandchildren. She lived in the house on Indianola Street for sixty-nine years. The wooden box that provided the entrance to the house had holes drilled through the steps so that it would not float away if the water rose. Children were advised not to ask as Grandmother did not wish to talk about it.

Erdmuthe only wanted peace and love. Because she carried these goals with her and shared them with others, she achieved her dream daily as she lived.

Daniel Shea saw his ambition for promotion thwarted when he signed his surrender and oath in 1865. He still saw his dream of heading a shipping company as viable. Ironically, the postwar expansion of Indianola as a shipping hub, which should have made his dream possible, practically ruled it out. The expansion was financed by large northern business interests that had no room for a rebel colonel. There were jobs as a ship captain, but he had done that before the war; pride and ambition prevented his stepping backward.

John Kittredge, honorable man, did not return to naval service when he was paroled by the Confederates. He became a customs inspector for the port of Boston. After the war, he saw bales of cotton arrive, headed for the New England mills. At the end of the day, he went home to his snug two-story house in Andover (fully paid for) to enjoy a view of the ocean and a pipe of tobacco.

John Ireland, who captured Kittredge, became the governor of Texas in 1882. He was strongly opposed to the land grants, which funded the westward expansion of railroads. His tenure as governor was a stormy one. Despite his opposition, the railroads pushed west and established the southern route to California, which Indianolans had viewed as great future for the port.

Will Moore and Erdmuthe's daughter, Frances Dickerson, married during the war and achieved her dream of family and his dream of commanding his own ship. In the postwar expansion, Will did indeed become a ship captain as his father before him, commanding a copper-sheathed, bronze-fastened schooner, the pride of the intracoastal shipping fleet. When the 1875 hurricane struck, Will, confident of his skill as a mariner, decided to save his ship by riding out the hurricane at sea. He lost the ship, but he and his mate survived. Hard work and dedication led to a second ship that survived the 1886 hurricane and was his livelihood thereafter.

Francis Williams, who was to be court-martialed in 1863, pursued his love of machinery diligently and eventually became the chief engineer of Morgan Shipping.

Samuel Clark, who jailed Bletchley and handled stragglers as he had his children, moved to Cuero in the 1875 exodus and died there in 1880.

Fort Esperanza was completely destroyed by the hurricane of 1875. All that was visible in later years were wooden supports and the infantry trenches.

* * *

About the Author

A retired engineer and university professor, he is the grandson of the main character of the book. The details of a Texas town which no longer exists were carefully researched to fill in the life of his predecessor during and just after the Civil War. Professor Dickerson is the author of two textbooks in the field of engineering.